Blessed Are You: Living the Beatitudes

Christopher J. Ruff, M.A., S.T.L.

Blessed Are You

Novo Millennio Press
1541 Old Hickory Drive
La Crescent, MN 55947
www.ChristopherRuff.com

Nihil obstat: Rev. Jesse D. Burish, S.T.L.
            Censor Librorum

Imprimatur: William Patrick Callahan, OFM Conv.
            Bishop of La Crosse
            January 14, 2018

The *nihil obstat* and *imprimatur* are official declarations that a book or pamphlet is free of doctrinal or moral error. No implication is contained therein that those who have granted the *nihil obstat* and *imprimatur* agree with the contents, opinions, or statements expressed.

Unless otherwise noted, Scripture quotations are from the Catholic Edition of the Revised Standard Version of the Bible, copyright © 1965, 1966 National Council of the Churches of Christ in the United States of America. Used by permission. All rights reserved.

Excerpts from the *Catechism of the Catholic Church,* Second Edition, for use in the United States of America, copyright © 1994 and 1997, United States Catholic Conference – Libreria Editrice Vaticana. Used by permission. All rights reserved.

Cover art:
Kenneth D. Dowdy, *Sermon on the Mount*
Used by permission. All rights reserved.

Graphics and Design:
Alice Andersen Socha

The Discipleship Series

Novo Millennio Press

The Beatitudes

Seeing the crowds, he went up on the mountain, and when he sat down his disciples came to him.

And he opened his mouth and taught them, saying:

> **"Blessed are the poor in spirit,**
> for theirs is the kingdom of heaven.

> **"Blessed are those who mourn,**
> for they shall be comforted.

> **"Blessed are the meek,**
> for they shall inherit the earth.

> **"Blessed are those who hunger and thirst for righteousness,**
> for they shall be satisfied.

> **"Blessed are the merciful,**
> for they shall obtain mercy.

> **"Blessed are the pure in heart,**
> for they shall see God.

> **"Blessed are the peacemakers,**
> for they shall be called sons of God.

> **"Blessed are those who are persecuted for righteousness' sake,**
> for theirs is the kingdom of heaven."

Matthew 5:1-10

Author's Note:

Jesus proclaimed eight Beatitudes in his Sermon on the Mount. For this book I have chosen to reflect on them in pairs in two instances:

- Session 1 reflects on "Blessed are the poor in spirit" and "Blessed are the meek."

- Session 3 reflects on "Blessed are those who hunger and thirst for righteousness" and "Blessed are those who are persecuted for righteousness' sake."

The remaining four Beatitudes are discussed in individual sessions.

Table of Contents

Session 4 – Recipients of God's Mercy, We are Called to be Merciful *(page 92)*

The Lord in His Scriptures
Catechism and Papal Quotes
The Lord in the Life of His People – *The Monk and the Murderer*
Questions for Discussion
Closing Prayer – *Prayer of St. Faustina*

Session 5 – A Heart Set on God *(page 116)*

The Lord in His Scriptures
Catechism and Papal Quotes
The Lord in the Life of His People – *The Mystical Heart of Brendan Kelly*
Questions for Discussion
Closing Prayer – *Psalm 51*

Session 6 – "Peace I Leave with You; My Peace I Give to You" *(page 138)*

The Lord in His Scriptures
Catechism and Papal Quotes
The Lord in the Life of His People – *An Impossible Peace (St. Teresa of Calcutta)*
Questions for Discussion
Closing Prayer – *Make Me a Channel of Your Peace*

Appendix – Suggestions for Service *(page 158)*

Blessed Are You: Living the Beatitudes

Introduction

Welcome to *Blessed Are You,* part of the Discipleship Series of small-group resources.

I wish to dedicate this book to Our Lady of Guadalupe, who first introduced me as a child to the wondrous, world-defying vision of the Beatitudes. Let me explain....

The Little Man and the Beautiful Lady

I was in the fourth grade when Sister Mary Michael told our class the story of St. Juan Diego and the beautiful Lady.[i] Juan Diego was a simple, native laborer, she said. He was passing through the countryside on his way to Mass when Our Lady appeared to him in a shining cloud on Tepeyac Hill, in what is now Mexico City, and entrusted to him a message. He was to go ask the bishop on her behalf to build a church at the place of the apparition.

The good Bishop Zumárraga gave Juan Diego an audience and listened kindly to his story. Not surprisingly, though, he was skeptical. As Juan set out for home, the beautiful Lady appeared to him again and he told her what had happened. "I beg you to entrust your message to someone more known and respected so that he will believe it," he said. "I am only a simple Indian whom you have sent as a messenger to an important person."

She replied, "My dearest son, you must understand that there are many more noble men to whom I could

---

Blessed Are You: Living the Beatitudes

Introduction

Welcome to *Blessed Are You,* part of the Discipleship Series of small-group resources.

I wish to dedicate this book to Our Lady of Guadalupe, who first introduced me as a child to the wondrous, world-defying vision of the Beatitudes. Let me explain....

The Little Man and the Beautiful Lady

I was in the fourth grade when Sister Mary Michael told our class the story of St. Juan Diego and the beautiful Lady.[i] Juan Diego was a simple, native laborer, she said. He was passing through the countryside on his way to Mass when Our Lady appeared to him in a shining cloud on Tepeyac Hill, in what is now Mexico City, and entrusted to him a message. He was to go ask the bishop on her behalf to build a church at the place of the apparition.

The good Bishop Zumárraga gave Juan Diego an audience and listened kindly to his story. Not surprisingly, though, he was skeptical. As Juan set out for home, the beautiful Lady appeared to him again and he told her what had happened. "I beg you to entrust your message to someone more known and respected so that he will believe it," he said. "I am only a simple Indian whom you have sent as a messenger to an important person."

She replied, "My dearest son, you must understand that there are many more noble men to whom I could

8

have entrusted my message and yet, it is because of you that my plan will succeed."

I was spellbound as Sister Mary Michael told us the rest of the story, culminating in the moment when Juan Diego opened before the bishop the folds of his tilma, his cloak, which concealed a bouquet of the finest Castilian roses. They had been lovingly arranged there by the Lady as a wondrous sign of her wishes, since it was impossible to find such roses in the dead of winter.

At once Bishop Zumárraga fell to his knees – but not at the sight of the roses tumbling out of the tilma. He was transfixed by the tilma itself, which now bore the miraculous image of the Mother of God.

What God Has Written in Our Hearts

Little boy that I was when I heard that story, I remember thinking, "Wow, this is like a fairy tale – only it's *true!*" It made me think of tales like Cinderella or the Ugly Duckling, in which lowly characters end up being the chosen ones. In this case little Juan Diego was chosen by 'the Queen,' Our Blessed Mother.

Isn't it remarkable that even while our fallen natures crave fame, fortune and power, something deep inside us celebrates at the sight of the humble, the poor and the lowly being lifted up? It appears God has wired us to rejoice at the truth conveyed by St. Paul: "God chose the foolish of the world to shame the wise, and God chose the

weak of the world to shame the strong, and God chose the
lowly and despised of the world, those who count for nothing, to reduce to nothing those who are something, so that
no human being might boast before God" (1 Cor:27-29).
This is the wonderful 'kingdom' of the Beatitudes,
and even our fairy tales hint at it!

Pale Replicas of the Original

St. Juan Diego exemplified the Beatitudes. He was
poor in spirit, meek, a man of peace and righteousness,
merciful in caring for a sick uncle, Juan Bernardino, and
full of holy mourning at the prospect of his uncle's im-
pending death (until Bernardino was miraculously cured
through Mary's intercession!).

And yet, even as we acknowledge St. Juan Diego as a
man of the Beatitudes, we must admit he is not their most
perfect embodiment. Neither are the graced men and
women whose stories are told in this book, though I have
hand-picked them to illustrate each of the Beatitudes.

No, we find the defining portrait of the Beatitudes in
the very Savior who proclaimed them, Jesus Christ. Born
in a stable to a poor virgin, persecuted by the powerful,
full of mercy for sinful, wounded humanity, weeping over
Jerusalem, divinely righteous yet "meek and humble of
heart," bestowing a peace the world cannot give – Jesus
is the ultimate Icon of the Beatitudes, compared to whom
even the greatest saint can only be a pale replica.

"O the Blessedness, O the Joy!"

In the Aramaic spoken by Jesus, the Beatitudes contained no verb. And so Jesus did not actually use a 'statement' formula, like "blessed *are* the poor in spirit," but rather a formula of exultation, of rejoicing – "O the blessedness of the poor in spirit," etc. Bible translators have added the verb in an effort to make the text more intelligible to our ears.

Language scholars also say that what we translate as "blessed" could equally be translated "happy." And so an alternative rendering would be, "O the happiness, O the blessed joy, of the poor in spirit, the merciful, the pure in heart...!"

Knowing all this, we can imagine the scene more vividly. From the Mount of the Beatitudes, Jesus looks lovingly at the crowd below, speaking to them from the fullness of his burning heart. He holds out to them a blessedness, a joy, that he yearns for them to share – and not just later in the glory of heaven, but even now in this world of light and shadow.

In the words of the renowned Scripture commentator William Barclay,

> The beatitudes in effect say, "O the bliss of being a Christian! O the joy of following Christ! O the sheer happiness of knowing Jesus Christ as Master, Saviour and Lord!" The very form of the beatitudes is the statement of the joyous thrill and the radiant gladness of the Christian life.[ii]

The Point of this Little Book

The goal of this book is to help those using it to let their hearts be opened and touched, so that they may drink deeply from the well of this joy – from the Living Water that is Jesus Christ – and live out the Beatitudes in their daily lives.

To help foster this goal, *Blessed Are You,* like the other books in the Discipleship Series, incorporates Scripture passages, snippets of wisdom from the Catechism and recent Popes, stories of men and women touched by grace, and prayers and discussion questions.

It also includes a modest component of service described on pages 16-17 and 158. This last element, with its focus on love of neighbor, comes from the conviction that true discipleship must take seriously Jesus' words, "Whatever you did for the least of my brethren, you did for me" (Mt 25:40).

I pray, dear reader, that we may all be made worthy vessels of the Beatitudes that leapt from the heart of the Son of God that day on the mountainside in Galilee. And as we strive to cooperate with God's grace, my thoughts turn again to the beautiful Lady of Guadalupe, to whom this book is dedicated. May her maternal gaze be upon us, and may she speak to us the words she directed that day in 1531 to one of the little ones of the Beatitudes, Juan Diego:

Listen and let it penetrate your heart.... Do not be troubled or weighed down.... Do not fear any illness or vexation, anxiety or pain. Am I not here who am your Mother? Are you not under my shadow and protection? Am I not your fountain of life? Are you not in the folds of my mantle? In the crossing of my arms? Is there anything else you need?

Christopher Ruff

i An excellent online source for more information on the apparitions of Our Lady of Guadalupe is: *https://www.ewtn.com/saintsHoly/saints/O/ourladyofguadalupe.asp*

ii William Barclay, *The Gospel of Matthew, Volume 2: New Daily Study Bible*, (Louisville, KY: Westminster John Knox Press, 2002) 102.

How to Use This Book

The Discipleship Series of small-group materials aims to be simple and flexible. What follows is everything you need to know to move forward:

Establishing and Running One or More Groups

- Form one or more small groups (5-12 people each) through personal invitation or parish announcements. For customizable bulletin inserts/flyers, visit www.ChristopherRuff.com and click on "Parish Launch Kit."

- If established for Lent, the groups should meet weekly. Otherwise, once a month tends to be more workable for most people's schedules. Typical length for a session is about 90 minutes. Whatever time frame is established, it should be rigorously respected.

- Each group should have a facilitator. It can be the same person at each meeting, or the facilitator role can rotate.

- The job of the facilitator is not to be an expert in the material or to do a lot of talking. Rather, it is to start and end the meeting on time, to help keep things moving and on topic, and to foster a friendly, supportive environment in which everyone feels invited to contribute.

- The group members decide where they would like to meet. It is ideal to hold the sessions in each other's homes since a key goal is to bring faith into daily life. If this is not workable, a room on church grounds is fine, or some combination of the two.

- Each member is expected to read the material prayerfully ahead of the session, jotting a few notes in response to the "Questions for Discussion."

- The session begins with the Prayer to the Holy Spirit or some other appropriate prayer so that hearts may be opened to God's presence.

- It is strongly recommended that the group members then read aloud the material for that session, taking turns reading a few paragraphs or a small section. This pattern should continue all the way through the discussion questions. Experience has shown this reading aloud to be not only do-able, but quite fruitful, making the material fresh and alive. The group may agree to strategically abbreviate the material to be read aloud if a session is particularly long or it is consuming too much time.

- When there are about ten minutes left in the allotted schedule, it is time to proceed to the "Group Prayers of Intercession," even if the group has not finished all the discussion questions.

- The prayers of intercession are intended to be spontaneous prayer intentions. They direct the power of prayer to various needs and

simultaneously deepen the spirit of fellowship in the group. Conclude with the "Closing
Prayer."

- The session should end on time, even if members are eager to keep going. This is vital for
the health and longevity of the group. It is
good to follow with fifteen or twenty minutes
of social time for those who are able to stay.
Simple refreshments are a nice touch, with
emphasis on the word simple; otherwise,
people feel pressure to keep up with high
expectations.

The Service Component

- The Service Component distinguishes this
program from many other small-group studies. It is anticipated that group members will
devote an hour or two to some form of service
between sessions (if meetings are weekly,
this could be an hour or two each month). The
service may be carried out individually or
together with others.

- Service can take many forms, but it should
come from the heart. Certainly service to the
poor, the sick, the elderly, the homebound,
the homeless, etc., has always had a privi-
leged place for Christ's followers.

- Some may already be devoting a great deal of
time to service. In that case, it is enough to
consciously "dedicate" some portion of that

service to the group's communal effort and spirit.

• Each set of "Questions for Discussion" includes at least one that touches on the component of service. This is to keep alive the awareness of the importance of the service aspect, which however is done on the "honor system" (with no one watching over anyone else's shoulder).

Group Etiquette

• Pray for the members of your group between sessions.

• Maintain confidentiality.

• Be a good listener and encourage everyone to contribute to the discussion, without anyone monopolizing. Members that are more talkative should allow everyone a chance to respond before they speak a second time.

• Love your neighbor by speaking charitably and refraining from any kind of gossip.

• Be on time, come prepared, and actively take part in discussion and prayer.

• Take seriously the service component so that you may be a loving (and always humble) witness to the others in your group.

• Be open and expect God's action in your life and prayer—expect to be changed!

Recommended prayer to start each session:

Prayer to the Holy Spirit

Come Holy Spirit,
Fill our hearts with the fire of your love.

Draw us near to Jesus,
so that we may witness to his presence
in every moment of our lives.

Renew us, so that our homes, parishes,
neighborhoods and world
may be transformed into the heavenly
Father's kingdom on earth,
where love and mercy reign.

Amen.

Session 1

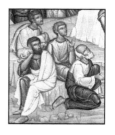

The Poverty That Makes Us Rich

> Blessed are the poor in spirit, for theirs is the kingdom of heaven....
> Blessed are the meek, for they shall inherit the earth.
>
> **Matthew 5:3,5**

The Lord in His Scriptures

The Blessed Poverty of the Tax Collector

[Jesus] told this parable to some who trusted in themselves that they were righteous and despised others:

"Two men went up into the temple to pray, one a Pharisee and the other a tax collector. The Pharisee stood and prayed thus with himself, 'God, I thank thee that I am not like other men, extortioners, unjust, adulterers, or even like this tax collector. I fast twice a week, I give tithes of all that I get.' But the tax collector, standing far off, would not even lift up his eyes to heaven, but beat his breast, saying, 'God, be merciful to me a sinner!' I tell you,

this man went down to his house justified rather than the other; for every one who exalts himself will be humbled, but he who humbles himself will be exalted."
Luke 18:9-14

Rich in the Things of God

"Therefore I tell you, do not be anxious about your life, what you shall eat or what you shall drink, nor about your body, what you shall put on. Is not life more than food, and the body more than clothing?

"Look at the birds of the air: they neither sow nor reap nor gather into barns, and yet your heavenly Father feeds them. Are you not of more value than they? And which of you by being anxious can add one cubit to his span of life? And why are you anxious about clothing? Consider the lilies of the field, how they grow; they neither toil nor spin; yet I tell you, even Solomon in all his glory was not arrayed like one of these. But if God so clothes the grass of the field, which today is alive and tomorrow is thrown into the oven, will he not much more clothe you, O men of little faith? Therefore do not be anxious, saying, 'What shall we eat?' or 'What shall we drink?' or 'What shall we wear?' For the Gentiles seek all these things; and your heavenly Father knows that you need them all. But seek first his kingdom and his righteousness, and all these things shall be yours as well."
Matthew 6:25-34

Meek and Humble of Heart

"Come to me, all you who labor and are burdened, and I will give you rest. Take my yoke upon you and learn from me, for I am meek and humble of heart; and you will find rest for yourselves. For my yoke is easy, and my burden light."[i]

Matthew 11:28-30

Soak in the Word

Two Minutes of Silence

Reflect...

The Gospels were written in Greek, and there were two words in Greek for "poor": *penés* and *ptóchos*. *Penés* referred to the "working poor," laborers of the lower class who struggled yet somehow managed to get by. But *ptóchos* referred to a much more radical kind of poverty, the poverty of beggars, of people driven to their knees, possessing nothing. Lacking any social standing, these beggars were utterly dependent on the generosity of others. Remarkably it is *this* word, *ptóchos,* that is used for the poor whom Jesus declares "blessed," or "happy."

What is he saying? Is Jesus advocating a life of destitution, of extreme material poverty? No, on the contrary, he calls on his disciples – then and now – to alleviate that kind of misery, to feed the hungry and clothe the naked.[ii] It is not material poverty that he is declaring blessed. Rather, "blessed are the poor *in spirit.*" Jesus is praising a state of mind and heart in relation to God. We are blessed if we understand that we come to God with empty hands, utterly dependent on him, like beggars or little children.

In the Parable of the Pharisee and the tax collector, we see that the tax collector acknowledges his poverty also in another way – as a sinner. He beats his breast and cannot even raise his eyes as he beseeches the Lord for mercy. Jesus leaves no doubt about the lesson of the parable: "Every one who exalts himself will be humbled, but he who humbles himself will be exalted" (18:14).

We should be poor in spirit in both these ways – in our complete, childlike dependence on God, and, like the tax collector, in the humble recognition that as sinners we depend particularly on his mercy and forgiveness. This should not depress us, but rather fill us with hope. The beautiful paradox is that it is precisely when we humbly fall on our knees and acknowledge our sinfulness and our dependence on God that we become open to the divine grace and love that "exalts" us, or literally "lifts us up." This is captured in the words of the Little Flower, St. Thérèse of Lisieux, as she reflects at the end of her life on the meaning of sanctity:

> Sanctity does not consist in this or that practice, it consists in a disposition of heart which makes us humble and little in the arms of God, conscious of our weakness and confident to the point of audacity in the goodness of the Father.... [Sanctity] is to recognize our nothingness, to expect everything from God as a little child expects everything from its father....[iii]

Of course, by God's grace, one member of the human race was poor in spirit *without* sin – the humble Virgin Mary. Her *Magnificat* (the closing prayer for this session), bursting with joy, glorifies God, recognizing that in his great mercy he has lifted her up from her lowliness, "scattered the proud," and "filled the hungry with good things!"[iv]

Hers is not a moral poverty. Mary does not need to beat her breast as a sinner. But she recognizes her littleness and utter dependence on the grace and providence of

God. She knows she has nothing of her own and must be cared for like the birds of the air and the lilies of the field. Her concern is not for herself, but for God and his kingdom.

The other Beatitude we have paired with "blessed are the poor in spirit" for this session is "blessed are the meek, for they shall inherit the earth." We have paired them because the meanings are very close and complementary. The only trouble is that in English the word "meek" is often taken to mean weak and passive, lacking in confidence and easily trampled upon. But that is not what is meant by the Greek word *praus* that we find in the Gospel of Matthew.

That Greek word carries several important connotations, including gentleness, humility and self-control. It is interesting to note also that it was used to describe domesticated animals obedient to their masters. Christian meekness, then, is docility to the Lord, humble responsiveness to the workings and directives of the Holy Spirit, with gentleness and self-control. We are to model our meekness, our docility, on that of Jesus, who said, "My food is to do the will of him who sent me."[v]

We see, then, how closely these two Beatitudes align, and once again we are struck by how beautifully they are embodied in the Blessed Virgin Mary. She was completely emptied of self and dependent on God, and she was perfectly docile to his direction. "Behold, I am the handmaid of the Lord. May it be done to me according to your word."[vi]

So what blessed assurance does Jesus give to those who are poor in spirit, to those who are meek? He assures them that the kingdom of heaven is theirs, and that they shall inherit the earth.

This is really two ways of saying the same thing. The kingdom of heaven exists wherever God reigns in the human heart. His kingdom has come wherever his will is done ("on earth, as it is in heaven"), and it will be unveiled in its full glory in the New Jerusalem, the heavenly city spoken of in Hebrews 11:16 and depicted in Revelation 21. It is this kingdom, this "new heaven and new earth," that belongs to us if we are poor in spirit, if we are meek and responsive to the Lord. It can belong to us even now, in the midst of the challenges and sufferings of this world, bringing us a blessed joy and peace that the world cannot take away.

Catechism of the Catholic Church

2547 – The Lord grieves over the rich, because they find their consolation in the abundance of goods.[vii] "Let the proud seek and love earthly kingdoms, but blessed are the poor in spirit for theirs is the Kingdom of heaven."[viii] Abandonment to the providence of the Father in heaven frees us from anxiety about tomorrow.[ix] Trust in God is a preparation for the blessedness of the poor. They shall see God.

Pope Benedict XVI

In his 2007 Christmas message, Pope Benedict XVI said faith and humility are needed to recognize the meaning of Jesus' birth. He noted the humility of those present:

The humility of Mary, who believed in the word of the Lord and, bending low over the manger, was the first to adore the fruit of her womb; the humility of Joseph, the just man, who had the courage of faith and preferred to obey God rather than to protect his own reputation; the humility of the shepherds, the poor and anonymous shepherds, who received the proclamation of the heavenly messenger and hastened towards the stable, where they found the new-born child and worshipped him, full of astonishment, praising God (cf. Lk 2:15-20). The little ones, the poor in spirit: they are the key figures of Christmas, in the past and in the present; they have always been the key figures of God's history, the indefatigable builders of his Kingdom of justice, love and peace *(Christmas Message, December 25, 2007).*

Pope Francis

In his message for the 29th World Youth Day, Pope Francis urged young people to imitate Christ in becoming poor in spirit, quoting St. Paul's letter to the Philippians:

"Have this mind among yourselves, which is yours in Christ Jesus, who, though he was in the form of God, did not count equality with God a thing to be grasped, but emptied himself, taking the form of a servant, being born in the likeness of men" (2:5-7).

Pope Francis continued:

Jesus is God who strips himself of his glory. Here we see God's choice to be poor: he was rich and yet he became poor in order to enrich us through his poverty (cf. 2 Cor 8:9). This is the mystery we contemplate in the crib when we see the Son of God lying in a manger, and later on the cross, where his self-emptying reaches its culmination *(Message of January 21, 2014)*.

The Lord in the Life of His People

"Thank God Ahead of Time"

*In every age, God raises up from among his humble
followers – from among the "poor in spirit" – holy men and
women who bear witness to him in extraordinary ways.
We usually think of them as figures at a distance from us
in time and space – Francis of Assisi, Vincent de Paul,
Thérèse of Lisieux. But the Spirit is always moving, even
in times and places that might surprise us. And so this is
the story of "Barney of Wisconsin" – otherwise known as
Blessed Solanus Casey.*

"Uh-oh, look who's coming."

The Capuchin friars who had been enjoying a moment of fellowship suddenly busied themselves as a tall,
thin friar with horn-rimmed glasses, bald head and long
gray beard approached, carrying his fiddle and bow. This
captive audience knew they were about to be serenaded
by Fr. Solanus Casey. Oh, they loved him dearly, but
that high, squeaky voice of his was like fingernails on a
chalkboard. They smiled and applauded a couple of times
before each discovered something he needed to do. And so,
as he sometimes did, Solanus made his way to the chapel,
where he finished playing before his Lord in the tabernacle.

God Chooses the Humble

Fr. Solanus Casey was the porter, or doorkeeper, at St. Bonaventure Monastery in Detroit. Ordained a priest in 1904, he could celebrate Mass, but his superiors had withheld from him the faculties of preaching and hearing confession because of poor academic performance during his formation. Solanus had accepted this decision in simple obedience. Everything seemed to point to a life of faithful, quiet obscurity, and if God had not had other plans, humble Solanus would have been quite content with that.

The sixth of sixteen children born to Irish immigrants, he came into the world on November 25, 1870, in Hudson, Wisconsin, and was named for his father, Bernard ("Barney") Casey. The Caseys were a devout farm family, and they filled their tiny log cabin with singing, stories and prayer, especially the rosary. The younger Barney worked hard on the farm until, at age 17, he left to supplement the family income through a variety of jobs, including lumberjack, prison guard and streetcar operator.

One day while driving his streetcar through a rough area of Superior, Wisconsin, Barney saw a woman brutally stabbed to death by a drunken, cursing sailor. This display of sheer evil shook him to the core and helped stir him, at the age of 21, to pursue a priestly vocation, entering the seminary in Milwaukee. It would be a winding and academically challenging path that saw him given the religious name "Solanus" and finally ordained a Capuchin priest at the age of 34.

Doorkeeper for the Lord

For his first assignment, Fr. Solanus was sent to Sacred Heart Parish in Yonkers, New York, where he served as sacristan and doorkeeper. He quickly became an ardent promoter of the Seraphic Mass Association, an apostolate of the Capuchins in which people would enroll and be remembered in the Masses, prayers, sacrifices and good works of the friars around the world.

When people came to Sacred Heart Parish seeking counsel, prayers for healing, etc., their first contact was the kind doorkeeper, Fr. Solanus, who, as soon as he got a whiff of their worries or woes, encouraged them to enroll in the Seraphic Mass Association. Suddenly stories began to circulate about miraculous cures and remarkable answers to prayer. For just over fifty years until his death in 1957, this "doorkeeper's ministry" would consume his life, in several different assignments, the longest of which returned him to St. Bonaventure's in Detroit where he had begun.

Solanus was directed to keep records of the "special favors" received by those who came to him for help, and by the end of his life these filled seven large notebooks. He would never take any credit though, always attributing the miracles to the Seraphic Mass Association. But the throngs that waited in line at the door – up to two hundred people each day – knew the hand of God was upon him. He encouraged many who came for help to go to confession, humbly referring them to another priest, since he had not received the faculty to hear confessions.

Time for Everyone, Care for the Poor

Brother Leo, a fellow friar at St. Bonaventure's, said that even though huge crowds waited for the chance to meet with Solanus, "he would never hurry anybody. He would listen to your story as if he had all the time in the world, and he would try to advise you, console you, comfort you and then he would usually give a blessing. When the people got home, often they would discover whoever had been sick was cured."[x]

But this extraordinary man was not a pious holy card figure. He loved to joke, played volleyball at recreation, enjoyed hot dogs piled high with onions, and was a baseball fan. He was also a man of profound social charity. His love for the poor inspired the Capuchins in Detroit to open a soup kitchen which became a major source of relief for poor eastside workers during the Depression. By 1931 the monastery soup kitchen was providing up to 3,500 free meals each day. Solanus spent a lot of time there, giving comfort to the hungry. One man, who became a dedicated kitchen volunteer, had come to him previously with a stomach tumor, asking for prayers. Solanus told him to go see his doctor again and then to come back and help feed the hungry. To the doctor's amazement, the tumor had disappeared.

Thank God Ahead of Time

Solanus believed that when making an appeal in prayer, we ought to "thank God ahead of time." He felt this showed such a level of grateful trust that it made it much harder for God to say no! He used this "prayer psychology" on the Blessed Mother, too. A woman named Gladys Feighan came to him one day, confiding her desire to have another child. She had had one baby, but then lost the next three due to a blood problem.

"You will have another child, Gladys," he said. "Your Blessed Mother will give you another child. You must believe this so strongly that before your baby is born you will get down on your knees and thank the Blessed Mother. Because once you ask her, and thank her, there's nothing she can do but go to her own Son and ask him to grant your prayer."[xi]

There were tears in his eyes as he spoke. Five years later, Gladys gave birth to twins.

Certainly many people who came to Fr. Solanus with prayer petitions did not see their petitions granted, and the good friar prepared them to bear their crosses. But in this and other cases of confident assurance, he was likely given the grace of special foreknowledge.

A Holy Death

Solanus lived to the advanced age of eighty-six. The day before his death from a long and painful skin ailment, he told his superior, Fr. Gerald Walker, "I looked on my whole life as giving, and I want to give until there is nothing left of me to give. So I prayed that, when I come to die, I might be perfectly conscious, so that with a deliberate act I can give my last breath to God."[xii]

The next morning his voice was weak and inaudible, until, as the attending nurse reported, he suddenly sat straight up in bed and said in a clear voice, 'I give my soul to Jesus Christ.' He died on July 31, 1957, precisely fifty-three years – to the day and to the hour – from his first Mass.

Twenty thousand people came to pay their last respects at Solanus Casey's viewing in Detroit. The opening of his cause for canonization was accepted by the Vatican in 1976. He was declared Venerable by Pope John Paul II in 1995 and beatified by Pope Francis in Detroit on November 18, 2017. It should come as no surprise that reports of miracles attributed to his intercession are plentiful, and continue to increase.

Questions for Discussion

1. Discuss what it means to be "poor in spirit" and "meek." In what ways do you see those Beatitudes evidenced in the story of Blessed Solanus Casey?

---

2. In declaring blessed those who are poor in spirit, Jesus clearly was referring to something deeper than material poverty, for it is possible to be rich in the world's goods yet remain poor in spirit, and it is possible to be materially poor yet greedy and self-centered. Still, we see Jesus in the Gospels invite a rich young man to sell all his possessions, give the money to the poor and follow him (cf. Lk 18:18-25). Saints throughout the ages have done exactly that (St. Francis of Assisi comes to mind) in imitation of Jesus, who possessed nothing. And members of religious congregations take a vow of poverty. So what kind of relationship do you think exists between these two things – poverty in spirit and the riches of this world?

_____

_____

_____

_____

_____

_____

_____

3. Discuss examples of people who have been meek and poor in spirit and the ways that was expressed in their lives. These could be figures from the Bible, saints or other well-known persons, or people in your own circle of family and acquaintances.

_____

_____

_____

_____

_____

_____

_____

_____

4. What sorts of practices, habits or attitude shifts might help you to better reflect these two Beatitudes in your own life?

_____

_____

_____

_____

_____

_____

_____

5. Discuss ways you might undertake the service com-
    ponent of this Discipleship Series program, whether
    individually or as a group, and how love of neighbor
    contributes to being poor in spirit.

_____

_____

_____

_____

_____

_____

_____

_____

Group Prayers of Intercession

8 to 10 minutes

Closing Prayer

The Magnificat

My soul magnifies the Lord,
and my spirit rejoices in God my Savior,
for he has regarded the low estate of his handmaiden.
For behold, henceforth all generations will call me
blessed;
for he who is mighty has done great things for me,
and holy is his name.
And his mercy is on those who fear him
from generation to generation.
He has shown strength with his arm,
he has scattered the proud in the imagination of their
hearts,
he has put down the mighty from their thrones,

41

and exalted those of low degree;

he has filled the hungry with good things,

and the rich he has sent empty away.

He has helped his servant Israel,

in remembrance of his mercy,

as he spoke to our fathers,

to Abraham and to his posterity for ever.

Amen.

Luke 1:46-55

i   New American Bible, copyright 1991, 1986, 1970, Confraternity of Christian Doctrine, Inc., Washington, D.C., and used by permission of the copyright owner. All Rights Reserved. No part of the New American Bible may be reproduced in any form without permission in writing from the copyright owner.

ii   Cf. Mt 25:35-36.

iii   St. Thérèse of Lisieux. *Last Conversations*, Trans. John Clark, OCD. (Washington, D.C.: ICS Publications, 1977) 129.

iv   Lk 1:51,53

v   Jn 4:34.

vi   Lk 1:38.

vii   Lk 6:24.

viii   St. Augustine, *De serm. Dom. in monte* 1,1,3:PL 34,1232.

ix   Cf. Mt 6:25-34.

x   Diane M. Hansen, "The Holy Doorman of St. Bonaventure: The Story of Venerable Solanus Casey." *The Word Among Us*. July 2011.

xi   Catherine Odell. *Solanus Casey: The Story of Father Solanus* (Huntington, IN: Our Sunday Visitor, 2007) 228.

xii   "Road to Sainthood." *Fr. Solanus Guild*, 2017. http://solanuscasey. org/who-is-father-solanus/road-to-sainthood.

Additional Works Consulted/Recommended:

Crosby, Michael, O.F.M., Cap. *Thank God Ahead of Time: The Life and Spirituality of Solanus Casey*. Cincinnati, OH: Franciscan Media, 2009.

Odell, Catherine. *Solanus Casey: The Story of Father Solanus*. Huntington, IN: Our Sunday Visitor, 2007.

Session 2

Holy Mourning

> Blessed are those who mourn, for they shall
> be comforted.
>
> **Matthew 5:4**

The Lord in His Scriptures

The Root of All Mourning

In the beginning was the Word, and the Word was
with God, and the Word was God.... In him was life, and
the life was the light of men.... He was in the world, and
the world was made through him, yet the world knew
him not. He came to his own home, and his own people
received him not.
John 1:1,3-4,10-11

The Tears of God

[W]hen he drew near and saw the city he wept over
it, saying, "Would that even today you knew the things

44

that make for peace! But now they are hid from your eyes. For the days shall come upon you, when your enemies will cast up a bank about you and surround you, and hem you in on every side, and dash you to the ground, you and your children within you, and they will not leave one stone upon another in you; because you did not know the time of your visitation."

Luke 19:37-44

Jesus Weeps at the Tomb of Lazarus

When the Jews who were with her in the house, consoling her, saw Mary rise quickly and go out, they followed her, supposing that she was going to the tomb to weep there. Then Mary, when she came where Jesus was and saw him, fell at his feet, saying to him, "Lord, if you had been here, my brother would not have died." When Jesus saw her weeping, and the Jews who came with her also weeping, he was deeply moved in spirit and troubled; and he said, "Where have you laid him?" They said to him, "Lord, come and see." Jesus wept.

John 11:31-35

Sorrow Will Turn to Joy

"A little while, and you will see me no more; again a little while, and you will see me.... Truly, truly, I say to you, you will weep and lament, but the world will rejoice; you will be sorrowful, but your sorrow will turn into joy. When a woman is in travail she has sorrow, because her

hour has come; but when she is delivered of the child, she no longer remembers the anguish, for joy that a child is born into the world. So you have sorrow now, but I will see you again and your hearts will rejoice, and no one will take your joy from you."
John 16:16, 20-22

They Shall be Comforted

Mary stood weeping outside the tomb, and as she wept she stooped to look into the tomb; and she saw two angels in white, sitting where the body of Jesus had lain, one at the head and one at the feet. They said to her, "Woman, why are you weeping?" She said to them, "Because they have taken away my Lord, and I do not know where they have laid him." Saying this, she turned round and saw Jesus standing, but she did not know that it was Jesus. Jesus said to her, "Woman, why are you weeping? Whom do you seek?" Supposing him to be the gardener, she said to him, "Sir, if you have carried him away, tell me where you have laid him, and I will take him away." Jesus said to her, "Mary." She turned and said to him in Hebrew, "Rab-bo'ni!"
John 20:11-16

He Will Wipe Away Every Tear

And I saw the holy city, new Jerusalem, coming down out of heaven from God, prepared as a bride adorned for her husband; and I heard a loud voice from the throne saying, "Behold, the dwelling of God is with men. He will dwell with them, and they shall be his people, and God himself will be with them; he will wipe away every tear from their eyes, and death shall be no more, neither shall there be mourning nor crying nor pain any more, for the former things have passed away." And he who sat upon the throne said, "Behold, I make all things new."
Revelation 21:2-5

Soak in the Word

Two Minutes of Silence

Reflect...

All the Beatitudes are paradoxical, but perhaps this one most of all. This is especially true when we recall that the Greek word for "blessed" is also translated "happy." Everyone knows that mourning is a form of sadness, so how can someone who is mourning be happy?

Or does Jesus mean that the blessedness of those who mourn is found not at all in mourning itself, but only in the assurance that God will eventually relieve the pain? That would make mourning itself simply an unfortunate affliction, like a headache. The only blessedness would be the good news that God has promised he will make it go away.

But no, mourning, as excruciating as it is, has dignity and value; it has something that makes it blessed even before the comfort comes. It is not just any kind of sadness. Rather, it is profound sorrow over a loss, often the loss of a beloved person through death.

Mourning thus *pays tribute* to what has been loved and lost. And the intensity of our mourning reveals the intensity of our love. As long as the object of our mourning is good and worthy, our mourning is blessed. It shows that our hearts are properly attuned. It would be a grave defect, a kind of curse, to fail to mourn the loss of a beloved spouse, a child, a dear friend. O unhappy the lot of the heart that is cold and unmoved in the face of such a loss!

When St. Padre Pio's mother died, he knew with a

supernatural awareness that she was in the state of grace and destined for heaven – yet he wept inconsolably, like a little child. Someone near him expressed surprise at this reaction from such a holy man. Padre Pio replied simply, "the heart has its part."

In the account of Jesus at the tomb of Lazarus, we see the blessedness of mourning in the tears of the very Son of God – even though he knew he would be raising Lazarus from the dead a few moments later. Perhaps God willed this detail in John's Gospel partly to show us that faith is not meant to be a vaccine against the emotions of the heart. Death is meant to be mourned, because God created us not to die but to live together forever. Our fallenness is at the root of death, and this separation brought by sin deserves our sorrow – indeed, it calls for this sorrow that pays tender tribute to the beloved.

So yes, there is blessedness in mourning itself. Of course that blessedness is incomplete until it is finally crowned by the ultimate comfort of heavenly reunion, where every tear is wiped away. But even now God comforts those who mourn. No one should ever feel alone in their mourning for, as Psalm 34 tells us, "The Lord is near to the brokenhearted."[i] He is near in moments of prayer and adoration. He is near in the sacraments, especially the Eucharist. And he is near through the love of other people.

Mourning is a worthy response whenever a profound good is lost (a loved one, health, home, employment), or whenever man's fundamental dignity is caused to suffer.

We mourn the hatred and bloodshed in the Middle East, the plight of the homeless and hungry man on the street, the desperation of a teenager being bullied, the loneliness of the bedridden woman in the nursing home, the tragedy of abortion and its victims.

And if we mourn properly, we continue to trust and hope in God, and we are also spurred to act, to bring loving help and relief to those whose pain we mourn, for in touching their wounds we touch the wounds of Christ.

This brings us to the most worthy and blessed mourning of all. St. Francis of Assisi experienced it, and it echoed in his cry of lamentation – "Love is not loved!" It is mourning at the world's rejection of God, a rejection that, by our sins, nailed our Savior to the cross. This is the theme especially of the first Scripture passage for this session (John 1:1,3-4,10-11).

Such sorrow pays tribute to a love beyond all other loves, and it has been felt by all the saints. St. Gemma Galgani, the saint profiled in this session, mourned intensely whenever she thought of her sins. She had such a vivid awareness of Jesus' love for her, a love reflected in every drop of blood he shed in his Passion. This meant that even her smallest faults caused St. Gemma deep sorrow.

Returning for a moment to the example of St. Francis, we discover that he could never have enough of meditating with tears of love on the sufferings of Christ. One of his biographers recounted the following incident:

> A young nobleman...found him one day utterly
> lost in sorrow. He addressed him, inquired the
> cause of his grief, and sought to comfort him. But
> his sorrow was not of earth, and earth had no con-
> solation for it. The Saint could only cry out, amidst
> his tears and sighs, 'Ah, if you would comfort me,
> let us weep together over the most bitter and most
> loving Passion of our Savior.'[ii]

And there we have the key that most perfectly un-
locks the paradox of this Beatitude. Yes, there is something good, noble and worthy in all true mourning, for it
pays tribute to love. But when the cause of our sorrow is
the suffering and death of Jesus Christ, our beloved Savior who died only that we might live, then mourning itself
is truly blessed and sweet, and we can say with St. Francis, "if you would comfort me, let us weep together...."

Catechism of the Catholic Church

1450 – "Penance requires . . . the sinner to endure all things willingly, be contrite of heart, confess with the lips, and practice complete humility and fruitful satisfaction."[iii]

1451 – Among the penitent's acts contrition occupies first place. Contrition is "sorrow of the soul and detestation for the sin committed, together with the resolution not to sin again."[iv]

1452 – When it arises from a love by which God is loved above all else, contrition is called "perfect" (contrition of charity).[v]

Pope Francis

How can those who weep be happy?

Those who have the ability to be moved, the ability to feel in their heart the pain in their lives and in the lives of others. These ones will be happy! Because the tender hand of God the Father will console and caress them *(Solemnity of All Saints, Nov. 1, 2015).*

Pope Benedict XVI

There are two kinds of mourning. The first is the kind that has lost hope.... But there is also the mourning occasioned by the shattering encounter with truth, which leads man to undergo conversion and to resist evil. This mourning heals, because it teaches man to hope and to love again. Judas is an example of the first kind of mourning: Struck with horror at his own fall, he no longer dares to hope and hangs himself in despair. Peter is an example of the second kind: Struck by the Lord's gaze, he bursts into healing tears that plow up the soil of his soul. He begins anew and is himself renewed[vi] *(Jesus of Nazareth,* p 86).

The Lord in the Life of His People

A Sorrow so Sweet

One of the aims of the Discipleship Series is to introduce, where appropriate, holy men and women who are not so well known. Such a one is St. Gemma Galgani, a 19th century Italian young lady who wept at the sufferings of Christ, prayed intensely for the conversion of sinners, and constantly extended herself to her neighbor in need. God had his eye on her from a tender age.

"All of a sudden, a voice in my heart said to me, 'Will you give me your Mamma?'"

"Yes," I answered, "if you will take me as well."

"No," the voice replied, "give me your Mamma without reserve. I will take you to heaven later."

"I could only answer 'Yes' and when Mass was over I ran home."[vii]

In the autobiography she wrote for her spiritual director, this is the exchange Gemma Galgani recalled having with Jesus on May 26, 1885, the day she was confirmed at the age of seven. It was the first of many mystical encounters she would have in her short lifetime.

Could we imagine any suffering more painful for a young child than to be invited to surrender her mother to death? Yet Gemma gave her "yes" and her mother died eighteen months later. This would be the first of many sorrows that she would embrace with a willing heart.

'Adorable' Gemma

Gemma was the fourth of eight children and the eldest daughter born to Enrico Galgani, a successful pharmacist, and his wife Aurelia, on March 12, 1878, in an Italian village just outside Lucca, near Florence. The couple was devoutly Catholic, and Aurelia in particular saw to the religious education of the children.

Gemma was an enchanting little girl. "Adorable" is the word we might use today. She had a beautiful round face, delicate features and an inner light that shone from her mature, tranquil eyes. Enrico doted on her. Upon getting home he would habitually ask, "Where is Gemma?" She was more conscious of this favoritism than he was, and from time to time took him to task, reminding him that he had other children!

When Gemma was two years old, she and her brothers and sisters were sent to a private school run by two eminent ladies of Lucca, Emilia and Elena Vallini. She attended the school for five years and the ladies later wrote of her:

> She was serious, thoughtful, wise in everything, and differed from all her companions. She was never seen to cry or to quarrel; her countenance was always calm and sweet. Whether petted or blamed, it was all the same, her only reply was a

modest smile, and her bearing was one of imper-
turbable composure. Her disposition was vivacious
and ardent, yet during her whole time with us we
were never obliged to punish her."[viii]

The ladies also noted that Gemma was diligent in her
studies and read easily from the Breviary by the age of
five. They wrote that all the children loved her, "especially
the little girls, who always longed to be with her."[ix]

In Love with the Suffering Jesus

Before her untimely death, Gemma's mother would
pray with her children morning and evening and taught
the older ones to make little meditations. Sometimes she
would take Gemma in her lap, point to the Crucifix and
say, "Look Gemma, how this dear Jesus died on the Cross
for us." Gemma would reply, "Tell me more, Mamma, tell
me more."

Gemma's eagerness to meditate on the Passion of
Christ would blossom further when, shortly after her
mother died, she was sent to a school run by the Sisters of
St. Zita in Lucca. Gemma later reflected:

I wanted to know all about the life and Passion of Jesus. I told my teacher of this desire and
she began, day by day, to explain these things to
me, choosing for this a time when the other children were in bed. She did this, I believe, without
the Mother Superior knowing of it. One evening
when she was explaining something to me about
the crucifixion, the crowning with thorns, and all
the sufferings of Jesus, she explained it so very

well that a great sorrow and compassion came over me. So much so that I was seized immediately with fever so intense that I was forced to remain in bed all the next day. From that day on the teacher explained such things only briefly.[x]

The Passion of Christ became, and remained, the very center of Gemma's life. In it she saw the ocean of God's love and the atrocity of sin which offended so great a love. God allowed her to behold her own sins in a vivid way, as if through his eyes. On one occasion she wrote to her spiritual director, Fr. Germano, "Yesterday evening I wept much at his feet. Oh how bitter were those tears, Father, and at the same time how sweet…. All my sins came to mind…. I felt greater sorrow for them than ever before…. But what consoles me is that I felt such great grief for them, and I would not wish this sorrow ever to be cancelled from my mind or ever to grow less."[xi]

Sorrow for Sin, Prayers for Sinners

When we read of the saints lamenting their sinfulness, we may shake our heads. Surely the sins of this lovely soul were not so great? But it is our own dullness to sin that throws us off. Most of us feel our sin like a grain of sand in our shoe. Gemma's sin was surely a much smaller "grain" – but she felt it as if in her eye. It caused her intense pain, but she welcomed that pain, and would not have had it any other way.

It was not only her own sins, but the sins of others that caused Gemma to grieve. One of her childhood teachers said, "I remember that when she was quite a small child she grieved if any of her companions acted wrongly….she prayed much, but especially for poor sinners, and offered for them such mortifications as a child can perform." This mission of reparation for sinners only grew stronger as her life progressed. She was consumed with longing for their salvation and begged God constantly to reach the hearts of sinners with his grace and mercy.

Here we must round out the portrait of Gemma Galgani, lest the impression be given that she was occupied solely with things unseen and mystical. While it is true that these were woven deeply into the fabric of her daily life, she took responsibility for the household in the manner expected of an eldest daughter whose mother had died, performing her tasks with great diligence.

A Heart for the Poor

Gemma also had extraordinary compassion for the sufferings of the poor and the sick. She wrote in her autobiography, "Every time I went out I used to ask father for money, and if, as sometimes happened, he refused I would take bread and flour and other things. And God arranged that I should often meet poor people, every time I left the house. To the poor who came to the door I gave clothes and whatever else I had."[xii]

Her Aunt Elisa wrote of Gemma:

> She often visited the sick in the hospital, to whom she brought a little money or something

else, and whom she comforted especially by speaking of God. She also overflowed with charity for the poor and used every means in her power to help them. Sometimes she would take something to an old man who lived at the corner of our street. At that time we ourselves were in reduced circumstances, so that I felt compelled to tell her, "There will be nothing left for our own supper." Gemma used to answer: "Providence will give us plenty." ...She also used to work for the poor, made them stockings and mended for them.[xiii]

One of the servants in the home of Gemma's rich aunt and uncle recalled the two of them walking along the road and meeting an old woman shivering from a lack of warm clothing. Gemma had just finished renovating a heavy under-skirt which had been given to her by her aunt. Seeing a sheltered doorway, Gemma entered it, removed the underskirt and gave it to the elderly woman, saying, "Pray for me that the Lord may set me on fire with his love."[xiv]

Mourning Sin to the Last

So much more could be written here about St. Gemma Galgani: about the several suitors who, seeing her beauty and grace, asked her to marry them; about her desire to be a nun, which would never be realized; about her sudden, miraculous cure from a deadly disease at the age of twenty-one; about the stigmata she received later that same year; and finally, about her months of agony culminating in her holy death at the age of twenty-five.

Through it all, Gemma maintained an extraordinary humility. Let us conclude with these words expressing her sense of unworthiness, yet her desire to belong only to Jesus.

"Oh, Jesus, how many sins? Do you not see them, Jesus? But Your mercy is infinite. You have forgiven me so many times, so forgive me once again. You know all, Jesus, You see my heart. You know, Jesus I am wholly Yours, all my body and soul. Let me suffer – yes, but I desire to be wholly Yours; I want to be in heaven with You."

Gemma Galgani died on April 11, 1903, after an agonizing illness, most likely tuberculosis. She was beatified by Pope Pius XI on May 14, 1933, and canonized by Pope Pius XII on Ascension Thursday, May 2, 1940.

Questions for Discussion

1. How is blessed mourning connected with love of God
    and love of neighbor?

---

2. What are some situations in our world today that
    summon us to mourning, as well as to action?

    _____

    _____

    _____

    _____

    _____

    _____

    _____

3. What types and situations of mourning did St. Gemma Galgani experience? Which were most intense and why?

_____

_____

_____

_____

_____

_____

_____

_____

4. In our life as Catholics, when and how do we express mourning, sorrow (don't only think of funerals)? How does each instance testify to love?

_____

_____

_____

_____

_____

_____

_____

5. This Beatitude says, "Blessed are those who mourn,
    for they will be comforted." In what ways does God
    comfort those who mourn? Have you experienced it?

_____

_____

_____

_____

_____

_____

_____

6. There is a connection between a person's capacity for
    proper mourning and his or her capacity for *true joy.*
    Where you find the one capacity, you find also the
    other. Discuss why this is so.

_____

_____

_____

_____

_____

_____

_____

Group Prayers of Intercession

8 to 10 minutes

Closing Prayer

Stabat Mater

At the cross her station keeping,
Stood the mournful mother weeping,
Close to Jesus to the last.

Through her heart, his sorrow sharing,
All his bitter anguish bearing,
Now at length the sword had passed.

Bruised, derided, cursed, defiled,
She beheld her tender child,
Till His Spirit forth he sent.

O, thou Mother, fount of love,
Touch my spirit from above,
Make my heart with thine accord.

Make me feel as thou has felt;
Make my soul to glow and melt
With the love of Christ our Lord.

Let me mingle tears with thee,
Mourning Him Who mourned for me,
All the days that I may live.

By the cross with thee to stay,
There with thee to weep and pray,
This I ask of thee to give.

Let me, to my latest breath,
In my body bear the death
Of that dying Son of thine.

Let us Pray:
Lord Jesus, as we mourn your Passion on Calvary,
May we mourn it also in the sufferings of our
neighbor in need,
Reaching out in love to the poor, the sick, the dying,
the lonely, the outcast,
Knowing that whatever we do for the least
of these your brethren,
We do for you. **Amen.**

i   Ps 34:18.

ii   Pamfilo de Magliano, *Life of St. Francis of Assisi*, (Whitefish, MT: Kessinger Publishing, 2010) 236.

iii   *Roman Catechism* II,V,21; cf. Council of Trent (1551): DS 1673.

iv   Council of Trent (1551): DS 1676.

v   Cf. Council of Trent (1551): DS 1677.

vi   Joseph Ratzinger. *Jesus of Nazareth*. (NY: Doubleday, 2007) 86.

vii Gemma Galgani, *Autobiography*. Website dedicated to St. Gemma Galgani, 2017. *www.stgemmagalgani.com/2008/11/autobiography-of-saint-gemma-galgani.html.*

viii Germanus Ruoppolo, C.P., *The Life of St. Gemma Galgani*. (Charlotte, NC:TAN, 2004) 2.

ix   Ibid., p. 3.

x   Galgani, op. cit.

xi   Ruoppolo, op. cit., p. 155.

xii Galgani, op. cit.

xiii Amedeo, C.P., *Biography of St. Gemma*. E-Catholic 2000, 2017. *www.ecatholic2000.com/galgani/amedeo.shtml.*

xiv Ibid.

Additional Works Consulted/Recommended:

Vast website devoted to St. Gemma Galgani: *www.stgemmagalgani.com.*

Session 3

The Eyes of the Lord are Upon the Righteous

> Blessed are those who hunger and thirst for righteousness, for they shall be satisfied.... Blessed are those who are persecuted for righteousness' sake, for theirs is the kingdom of heaven.
>
> **Matthew 5:6,10**

The Lord in His Scriptures

Foreshadowing the Persecution of Christ, the Righteous One

...[U]ngodly men by their words and deeds summoned death;
"Let us lie in wait for the righteous man,
because he is inconvenient to us and opposes our actions;
he reproaches us for sins against the law,
and accuses us of sins against our training.
He professes to have knowledge of God,
and calls himself a child of the Lord.
He became to us a reproof of our thoughts;
the very sight of him is a burden to us,

70

because his manner of life is unlike that of others,
and his ways are strange.
We are considered by him as something base,
and he avoids our ways as unclean;
he calls the last end of the righteous happy,
and boasts that God is his father.
Let us see if his words are true,
and let us test what will happen at the end of his life;
for if the righteous man is God's son, he will help him,
and will deliver him from the hand of his adversaries.
Let us test him with insult and torture,
that we may find out how gentle he is,
and make trial of his forbearance.
Let us condemn him to a shameful death,
for, according to what he says, he will be protected."
Wisdom 1:16; 2:1,12-20

1 Peter on Christian Righteousness

"He that would love life and see good days, let him
keep his tongue from evil and his lips from speaking guile;
let him turn away from evil and do right; let him seek
peace and pursue it. For the eyes of the Lord are upon the
righteous, and his ears are open to their prayer. But the
face of the Lord is against those that do evil."[i]

Now who is there to harm you if you are zealous for
what is right? But even if you do suffer for righteousness'
sake, you will be blessed. Have no fear of them, nor be

troubled, but in your hearts reverence Christ as Lord.

Always be prepared to make a defense to anyone who calls you to account for the hope that is in you, yet do it with gentleness and reverence; and keep your conscience clear, so that, when you are abused, those who revile your good behavior in Christ may be put to shame. For it is better to suffer for doing right, if that should be God's will, than for doing wrong. For Christ also died for sins once for all, the righteous for the unrighteous, that he might bring us to God, being put to death in the flesh but made alive in the spirit....

1 Peter 3:10-18

Joseph, Upright Husband of Mary

Now the birth of Jesus Christ took place in this way. When his mother Mary had been betrothed to Joseph, before they came together she was found to be with child of the Holy Spirit; and her husband Joseph, being a just man and unwilling to put her to shame, resolved to divorce her quietly.

But as he considered this, behold, an angel of the Lord appeared to him in a dream, saying, "Joseph, son of David, do not fear to take Mary your wife, for that which is conceived in her is of the Holy Spirit; she will bear a son, and you shall call his name Jesus, for he will save his people from their sins."

All this took place to fulfil what the Lord had spoken by the prophet: "Behold, a virgin shall conceive and bear a son, and his name shall be called Emmanuel" (which means, God with us). When Joseph woke from sleep, he did as the angel of the Lord commanded him.
Matthew 1:18-24

Soak in the Word

Two Minutes of Silence

Reflect...

Our first Scripture passage, from the Old Testament book of Wisdom, clearly foreshadows what would happen to Jesus, the ultimate Righteous One. It is easy to picture these conniving words on the lips of the leaders who so envied and hated Jesus that they plotted to kill him. In fact, in Matthew's account of the Passion, the chief priests, the scribes and the elders echo words from this passage at the foot of the cross, as they cry out in mockery: "He trusts in God; let God deliver him now, if he desires him; for he said, 'I am the Son of God.'"[ii]

We must bear in mind that the persecution of the righteous reflected in this passage from the book of Wisdom applies not just to Jesus, but – to one degree or another – to anyone who seeks to follow him. Recall what he told his disciples the night before he died: "If the world hates you, know that it has hated me before it hated you. If you were of the world, the world would love its own; but because you are not of the world, but I chose you out of the world, therefore the world hates you. Remember the word that I said to you, 'a servant is not greater than his master.' If they persecuted me, they will persecute you...."[iii]

Should we be surprised, then, by the often twisted way "the world" looks at those who are trying to lead righteous lives? Should we be shocked to see Christians who adhere to Judeo-Christian morality persecuted as "backward" and "haters," especially if they dare to make their convictions known and to live by them both privately and publicly? This persecution may come at times even from family members or persons we thought of as friends, making it all the more painful. See the quote below from Pope St. John Paul II about what he describes as "hidden martyrdom" in this regard.

We should be consoled, though, by the passage from the first letter of Peter. Those beautiful words should instill in us a sense of peace as we seek to live righteously, even if we are criticized or misunderstood. They remind us not to give in to feeling troubled or afraid, but to entrust ourselves entirely to Christ, ready always to give a reason for the hope that sustains us, but with gentleness.

Finally, there can scarcely be a discussion of righteousness without referring to St. Joseph, the "just man" whom God chose to be the husband of Mary and the foster father of Jesus. We know little of him from Scripture, except that whatever God asked of him, he did without hesitation, whether taking Mary as his wife or fleeing into Egypt with the Holy Family when an angel warned him of Herod's plot to murder Jesus.[iv] We can always turn to righteous St. Joseph in our own times of trial.

Catechism of the Catholic Church

1989 – The first work of the grace of the Holy Spirit is conversion, effecting justification in accordance with Jesus' proclamation at the beginning of the Gospel: "Repent, for the kingdom of heaven is at hand."[v] Moved by grace, man turns toward God and away from sin, thus accepting forgiveness and righteousness from on high.

Pope Benedict XVI

The people this Beatitude describes ["Blessed are those who hunger and thirst for righteousness..."] are those who are not content with things as they are and refuse to stifle the restlessness of heart that points man to something greater and so sets him on the inward journey to reach it – rather like the wise men from the East seeking Jesus, the star that shows the way to truth, to love, to God[vi] *(Jesus of Nazareth,* p. 91).

Pope St. John Paul II

A believer "suffers for righteousness' sake" when, in exchange for his fidelity to God, he experiences humiliations, maltreatment, derision from his own, and misunderstanding even from the persons dearest to him. When he exposes himself to opposition, he risks unpopularity or other unpleasant consequences. Yet he is always ready for any sacrifice, since "we must obey God rather than men."[vii] Alongside public martyrdom, which takes place before the eyes of many, how often does a hidden martyrdom take place in the depths of people's hearts *(Homily in Bydgoszcz, Poland, June 7, 1999).*

Pope Francis

Why does the world persecute Christians? The world hates Christians for the same reason that they hated Jesus: because he brought the light of God, and the world prefers darkness so as to hide its evil works. Let us recall that Jesus himself, at the Last Supper, prayed that the Father might protect us from the wicked worldly spirit. There is opposition between the Gospel and this worldly mentality *(Angelus address on Dec. 26, 2016, Feast of St Stephen, first martyr).*

The Lord in the Life of His People

Blessed Padre Pro: Righteous to the End

The story of Blessed Miguel Pro reveals the love and good humor of a priest who courageously embraced his ministry to his people, especially the little and the poor. He did so in the face of danger, persecution and ultimately death.

As the train lurches forward, a young priest steadies himself and ducks into a compartment to sit down. Seated around him he sees a collection of rugged coal miners. The men glance at him and then at one another with sour expressions. The priest takes no notice and cheerfully strikes up a conversation. The place is Belgium, the year 1925, eight years after Vladimir Lenin has scattered the seeds of Communism from his "October Revolution" in Russia.

"I, too, am a Communist!"

One of the men gruffly interrupts the young priest's pleasantries. "Father, we are all socialists."

"Ah, marvelous!" comes the priest's immediate reply, "for I too am a socialist, but not in the same way. Do you really know what the word means? Who can tell me?"

After an uneasy pause and some halting efforts, one of the men says the work of socialists is "to take money from the rich."

"Ah, I see" says the priest, with a twinkle in his eye. "But once we have all that money, how will we be able to protect it from thieves?"

A couple of the men chuckle, but one asks, "Aren't you afraid of us?" He then adds, in a menacing tone, "Some of us are Communists."

"Even better," he replies, "for I, too, am a Communist. It is one o'clock, and I am hungry. I see that some of you are eating, and surely as good Communists you will want to share your food with me."

Now all the men laugh, but one persists with the question, "Why weren't you afraid to come in here?"

"Because," he replies, "I am always well armed."

Eyebrows raised in surprise, the men ask to see his weapon. He reaches into his pocket and draws out a crucifix. "Here it is. With the Lord at my side, I have nothing to fear."

At the sight of the crucifix, several of the rough coal miners reverently remove their hats. The priest uses the remaining minutes before the next stop to explain why the Lord is much more effective than a pistol. As the train slows and the men get up to leave, one of them thrusts a bag into his hand. The priest smiles as he opens it, seeing a gift of chocolates.

Born for this

This was a classic episode in the life of Fr. Miguel Pro – "Padre Pro." The third of eleven children born to mining engineer Miguel Pro and his pious wife Josefa Juarez, he came into the world on January 12, 1891, in the Mexican village of Guadalupe Zacatecas. From early childhood he was spirited and comical, a lover of practical jokes.

Miguelito ("little Miguel") did not seem as obviously pious as his two older sisters, both of whom would enter religious life while he was yet a boy. But he participated gladly in family devotions and benefited from the witness of Christian charity given by his good father and mother.

Miguel's mother was especially well known for her compassion for the sick and the poor, bringing them food and medicines. She even established a free hospital for those who could not otherwise afford medical care.

Following the entry of his two older sisters in religious life, Miguel discerned his own calling to the priesthood, joining the Jesuits in 1911. He studied in Mexico until 1914, when a tidal wave of governmental anti-Catholicism crashed down upon his country, forcing the novitiate to disband and the order to flee to Los Gates, California.

Over the next decade, his formation would take him not only to the United States, but also Spain, Nicaragua and Belgium, where he was ordained in 1925. In Belgium he often visited the miners in the town of Charleroi. He witnessed their miserable working and living conditions,

80

and this sharpened in him the need to be near the suffering and exploited and to dedicate himself to their welfare.

Wherever he went, Padre Pro was known for his playful spirit, but also his deep piety. When he first made his vows with the Jesuits, he wrote in a spiritual notebook: "Deceitful are the ephemeral pleasures and joys of this world. Our supreme comfort in this life is to die to the world that we may live with Jesus crucified. Let others seek gold and other earthly treasures. I already possess the immortal treasure of holy poverty on the Cross of Jesus crucified."

A Wave of Persecution vs. a Master of Disguise

Young Padre Pro suffered greatly from a severe stomach ailment and when after several operations his health did not improve, in 1926 his superiors gave him permission to return to Mexico in spite of what had now become a raging anti-religious persecution in the country. All Catholic churches were closed. Bishops and priests were rounded up for deportation or imprisonment. Those caught trying to minister in secret were shot. Celebration of the sacraments was punishable by imprisonment or death. The Church was driven underground.

In the midst of all this, Padre Miguel quietly slipped into Mexico City and immediately began celebrating Mass and the Sacraments, often under imminent threat of discovery by the police. A master of disguise, his narrow escapes were as creative – and at times comical – as they were dangerous.

Once, after celebrating Mass in a home, Padre Pro was tipped off that the police were coming. Slipping out just before they arrived, he changed into a police inspector's uniform (one of his many disguises) and swaggered back into the house. He went straight to the policeman in charge and demanded to know why they hadn't succeeded in capturing "that rascal Pro." The embarrassed chief officer vowed, "We will get him yet!"

Another time, with the police hot on his trail, the young Padre jumped into a taxi and told the driver to take off. Looking in the rearview mirror, he told the driver to round a corner. At that instant he rolled out the door, lit a cigar and began walking arm in arm with a startled young woman he had spotted on the sidewalk. The police roared past in pursuit of the taxi, paying no attention to the lovely young couple out for a stroll.

Padre Pro became known throughout Mexico City as the undercover priest who would show up in the middle of the night, dressed as a beggar or a street sweeper, to baptize infants, hear confessions, distribute Communion, or celebrate marriages. His personal writings from that time bear witness to his loving ministry to truck drivers, to poor women exploited into prostitution, to university students and professionals, to anyone wishing to deepen their devotion to Jesus in this time of persecution.

A Martyr's Cry: "Viva Cristo Rey!"

The young Padre was fearless in the face of the constant efforts to capture him. Completely trusting in God's providence, he wrote, "The most that those fellows can do to me is kill me; but this will not happen except on the day and the hour that the good God chooses.... The dangers among which we live are terrible. Terrible if we look at them with the eyes of the body, but not so if we look at them with the eyes of the soul."

In November 1927 there was a failed assassination attempt on General Alvaro Obregón, a former President of Mexico. Padre Pro and two of his brothers, Humberto and Roberto, were captured and arrested on false charges of being involved. They were imprisoned and sentenced to death, even after another man confessed to the attempt and testified that the Pro brothers had nothing to do with it. Roberto was eventually released, but Padre Pro would meet the martyr's destiny for which he had prepared his soul, as would his brother Humberto.

As his turn came to stand before the firing squad, Padre Pro blessed the soldiers, knelt and prayed quietly for a few moments. Declining a blindfold, he faced his executioners with a crucifix in one hand and a rosary in the other, arms outstretched as if on a cross. He exclaimed, "May God have mercy on you! May God bless you! Lord, you know that I am innocent! With all my heart I forgive my enemies!" Before the firing squad was ordered to shoot, Pro raised his arms in imitation of Christ and shouted, *Viva Cristo Rey!* – "Long live Christ the King!" After the volley from the firing squad knocked him to the ground, a soldier shot him at point-blank range to assure his death.

A Hero Forever

President Calles had Padre Pro's execution photographed and published the pictures as a warning to anyone who would consider following in his footsteps. But Calles' action had the opposite effect. That evening and the next day a continual stream of visitors poured into the family home to pay their respects before the coffins of the two brothers. A throng of 40,000 is reported to have lined Padre Pro's funeral procession, as flowers showered down from open windows and people knelt in the streets to revere the passing body of their hero and martyr. Another 20,000 waited at the cemetery where he was buried without a priest present, his father saying the final words.

Persecution and anticlericalism would persist for decades in Mexico, and still today we see efforts to suppress the influence of religion on public life. But in the land of Our Lady of Guadalupe, Christian devotion burns bright in the hearts of the masses and Padre Pro remains a hero. He was beatified as a martyr for the Faith by Pope St. John Paul II on September 25, 1988.

Questions for Discussion

1. In the passage from the book of Wisdom that opens
   this session, we find this said of the righteous man:
   "He became to us a reproof of our thoughts; the very
   sight of him is a burden to us."[viii] Why is it that the
   very presence of a righteous person can disturb people? Have you ever seen this?

2. When you think of righteousness, who are some examples that come to mind, and why?

_____

_____

_____

_____

_____

_____

_____

3. The 21st Century has had far too many examples of the persecution of Christians. Think about how you might be able to help our brothers and sisters who are too often forced out of their homes or even killed for being followers of Christ. Visit the website of Aid to the Church in Need (www.churchinneed.org) and discuss what you learn there.

_____

_____

_____

_____

_____

_____

_____

_____

4. In the quote from Pope Benedict XVI, he talks about those who hunger and thirst for righteousness as being "not content with things as they are" and having "restlessness of heart." Why is this a good thing, and in what way is it similar to the blessedness of those who mourn?

_____

_____

_____

_____

_____

_____

_____

5. What did you particularly appreciate or enjoy about the profile of Blessed Padre Pro? What do you see in him that you would especially like to emulate?

_____

_____

_____

_____

_____

_____

_____

_____

Group Prayers of Intercession

8 to 10 minutes

Closing Prayer

Knights of Columbus Prayer for Persecuted Christians

O God of all the nations,
The One God who is and was and always will be,
In your providence you willed that your Church
Be united to the suffering of your Son.

Look with mercy on your servants
Who are persecuted for their faith in you.
Grant them perseverance and courage
To be worthy imitators of Christ.

Bring your wisdom upon leaders of nations
To work for peace among all peoples.
May your Spirit open conversion
For those who contradict your will,
That we may live in harmony.

Give us the grace to be united in truth and freedom,

And to always seek your will in our lives.

Through Christ our Lord. Amen.

Our Lady, Queen of Peace, pray for us.

Prayer composed by Archbishop William E. Lori,
Supreme Chaplain of the Knights of Columbus

---

i   Cf, Psalm 34:12-16.

ii   Mt 27:43.

iii Jn 15:18-20.

iv Cf, Mt 3:13.

v   Mt 4:17.

vi Joseph Ratzinger. *Jesus of Nazareth.* (NY: Doubleday, 2007) 91.

vii Acts 5:29.

viii Wis 21:14,15

Additional Works Consulted/Recommended:

Ball, Ann. *Blessed Miguel Pro: 20th Century Martyr.* Charlotte, NC: TAN, 1996

Molinari, Paolo, S.J., "*Il Beato Michele Agostino Pro, Martire della Fede.*" *La Civiltà Cattolica,* 1988, IV, 128-140, translated by José María Fuentes, S.J. for the Center for Ignatian Spirituality, Manila Philippines.

Session 4

Recipients of God's Mercy, We are Called to be Merciful

> Blessed are the merciful, for they shall obtain mercy.
>
> **Matthew 5:7**

The Lord in His Scriptures

Yahweh's Command: Mercy toward the Afflicted

Is not this the fast that I choose: to loose the bonds of wickedness, to undo the thongs of the yoke, to let the oppressed go free, and to break every yoke? Is it not to share your bread with the hungry, and bring the homeless poor into your house; when you see the naked, to cover him, and not to hide yourself from your own flesh? Then shall your light break forth like the dawn, and your healing shall spring up speedily; your righteousness shall go before you, the glory of the LORD shall be your rear guard. Then you shall call, and the LORD will answer; you shall cry, and he will say, Here I am.

If you take away from the midst of you the yoke, the pointing of the finger, and speaking wickedness, if you pour yourself out for the hungry and satisfy the desire of the afflicted, then shall your light rise in the darkness and your gloom be as the noonday. And the LORD will guide you continually, and satisfy your desire with good things, and make your bones strong; and you shall be like a watered garden, like a spring of water, whose waters fail not.
Isaiah 58:6-11

The Woman Caught in Adultery

Early in the morning [Jesus] came again to the temple; all the people came to him, and he sat down and taught them. The scribes and the Pharisees brought a woman who had been caught in adultery, and placing her in the midst they said to him, "Teacher, this woman has been caught in the act of adultery. Now in the law Moses commanded us to stone such. What do you say about her?"

This they said to test him, that they might have some charge to bring against him. Jesus bent down and wrote with his finger on the ground. And as they continued to ask him, he stood up and said to them, "Let him who is without sin among you be the first to throw a stone at her." And once more he bent down and wrote with his finger on the ground.

But when they heard it, they went away, one by one,

beginning with the eldest, and Jesus was left alone with the woman standing before him. Jesus looked up and said to her, "Woman, where are they? Has no one condemned you?"

She said, "No one, Lord." And Jesus said, "Neither do I condemn you; go, and do not sin again."
John 8:2-11

Mercy without Limit

Then Peter came up and said to him, "Lord, how often shall my brother sin against me, and I forgive him? As many as seven times?" Jesus said to him, "I do not say to you seven times, but seventy times seven."
Matthew 18:21-22

Soak in the Word

Two Minutes of Silence

Reflect...

Mercy has been a central theme in the life of the Church in recent decades. It was a special focus of Pope St. John Paul II, who made it the subject of an encyclical, canonized St. Faustina Kowalska, recipient of the Divine Mercy messages, and declared the Sunday after Easter Divine Mercy Sunday. It has also been central to Pope Francis, who proclaimed a Holy Year of Mercy in 2015.

Arguably the most profound and beautiful papal reflection on mercy is Pope St. John Paul II's 1980 Encyclical *Dives in Misericordia* ("Rich in Mercy"). He writes that mercy is that form of love that tenderly comes to the aid of one who is suffering. That suffering may be physical or emotional, or it may be the moral misery that comes from having sinned.

In the first sense – that of mercy shown in the context of physical and emotional suffering – we consider the passage above from Isaiah. Yahweh commands his Chosen People to show mercy to the hungry, the homeless, the naked, the oppressed. He calls them to practice what we have come to know as the "corporal works of mercy." Jesus will raise this summons to new heights in Matthew 25, telling his disciples that this mercy shown to "the least of these my brethren" will be decisive at the Last Judgement. There are countless examples in the Gospels in which he shows this form of mercy – healing lepers, restoring sight to the blind, making the lame walk, even raising the dead.

The second sense – that of mercy shown in the context of moral misery – is seen in the passages from the Gospels of John and Matthew. As painful as physical and emotional suffering may be, the damage caused by sin is far more deadly. It afflicts the soul, darkening the image of God in us. When it is grave ("mortal"), sin jeopardizes our very salvation. So it is this mercy toward sinners that lies at the very heart of Jesus' mission. He has come to raise us from death to new life, even those guilty of the most heinous sins, as we shall see in this session's profile, "The Monk and the Murderer."

This mercy that restores sinners to grace is not cheap or sentimental. It comes at the cost of Jesus' agony and death on the Cross; it also requires the sinner to repent and resolve to amend his or her life. Jesus forgives the woman caught in adultery, yes, but his last words to her are, "go and sin no more." Recall, too, that the prodigal son of the famous parable receives his father's merciful embrace only after recognizing his sin and resolving to return repentant to his father's house. As St. John Paul II wrote about the infinite power of God's mercy: "No human sin can prevail over this power or even limit it. On the part of man only a lack of good will can limit it, a lack of readiness to be converted and to repent."[i]

Our final passage has Peter asking the Lord how often he must forgive someone who sins against him – seven times? The rabbis in Jesus' day held that one must be ready to forgive an offender three times, so Peter probably thought he was being generous by more than doubling that number. Jesus' response dwarfs Peter's proposal.

"Seventy times seven" is not meant to be an exercise in mathematics, but to tell us that we must be ready to forgive beyond all counting. After all, that is what God does for us. Consider how often we confess the same sins in the Sacrament of Reconciliation. And recall Jesus' admonition that the measure with which we forgive others will be the measure according to which God will forgive us (see the parable of the unforgiving servant[ii]).We underscore this reality every time we say in the Lord's Prayer: "Forgive us our trespasses, as we forgive those who trespass against us."

Catechism of the Catholic Church

2447 – The *works of mercy* are charitable actions by which we come to the aid of our neighbor in his spiritual and bodily necessities. Instructing, advising, consoling, comforting are spiritual works of mercy, as are forgiving and bearing wrongs patiently. The corporal works of mercy consist especially in feeding the hungry, sheltering the homeless, clothing the naked, visiting the sick and imprisoned, and burying the dead. Among all these, giving alms to the poor is one of the chief witnesses to fraternal charity.

Pope Francis

God's mercy can make even the driest land become a garden, can restore life to dry bones (cf. Ez 37:1-14). ...Let us be renewed by God's mercy, let us be loved by Jesus, let us enable the power of his love to transform our lives too; and let us become agents of this mercy *(Easter message, March 31, 2013)*.

Pope St. John Paul II

...[M]ercy becomes an indispensable element for shaping mutual relationships between people.... It is impossible to establish this bond between people, if they wish to regulate their mutual relationships solely according to the measure of justice. In every sphere of interpersonal relationships justice must, so to speak, be "corrected" to a considerable extent by that love which...is so much of the essence of the Gospel and Christianity.... [M]erciful love is supremely indispensable between those who are closest to one another: between husbands and wives, between parents and children, between friends *(Dives in Misericordia, 14)*.

[L]ove is present in the world and...is more powerful than any kind of evil in which individuals, humanity, or the world are involved. Believing in this love means believing in mercy. For mercy is an indispensable dimension of love; it is as it were love's second name *(Dives in Misericordia, 7)*.

The Lord in the Life of His People

The Monk and the Murderer

The following story is an abridged version of the article, "The Monk and the Murderer," by Annie Calovich. A testimony to the miraculous power of mercy, it is reprinted with the author's permission.

Brother Vianney-Marie Graham of the contemplative Clear Creek Monastery in Hulbert, Oklahoma, had long been praying for inmates on Death Row because he considered them "the abandoned of the abandoned."

He had a famous precedent for his prayers. St. Thérèse of Lisieux had prayed for the conversion of the notorious and unrepentant killer Henri Pranzini in 1887 and was able to read in the newspaper of his last-minute grab for a crucifix as he approached the scaffold. He kissed the wounds of Jesus three times before being guillotined.

In 2001, Brother Vianney-Marie decided to ask his superior for permission to write a few inmates, "to tell them not to despair, to tell them that God's mercy is available to them no matter what their crimes."

In deciding whom to write, Brother Vianney-Marie sought out the worst cases. He started with James Malicoat, a man who had brutally killed his 13-month-old daughter through a series of beatings over two weeks.

"When I first saw the crime, I thought, 'He needs a

friend more than the others. Everyone is going to shrink back because the crime was so horrendous,'" Brother Vianney-Marie said.

He received permission from his superior to write to Malicoat, and did so for the first time on the feast of the Assumption, 2001. Malicoat took a month and a half to respond, dating his letter October 1, which is the feast of St. Thérèse.

Brother Vianney-Marie wrote faithfully to Malicoat and two other inmates once a month for two years. Then he received permission to go to Death Row once a year to visit them.

Visits to Death Row

He first met Malicoat on Sept. 17, 2003. The inmate at first hesitated to talk about his crime. He said he was afraid of scandalizing the monk. But eventually, after Brother Vianney-Marie told him stories of the despairing people he used to work with at a factory before entering religious life, Malicoat unloaded a tale he'd bottled up for years.

Malicoat didn't know why he killed his daughter, named Tessa. He had been beaten as a child. He didn't know for sure who his father was. He was married but had been living with another woman, the mother of his child, when Tessa died of her injuries on February 21, 1997. The mother was serving a life sentence for allowing the torture.

"Until that moment, he had been five years on Death Row and hadn't spoken to anyone about his crime," Brother Vianney-Marie said. He could see that the unburdening was a great relief to Malicoat. And then the monk thought to ask a question that might get deeper into the killer's mind and open it up.

"Do you talk to Tessa?"

The look of shock that passed over Malicoat's face — the only time Brother Vianney-Marie had seen him emotional — told the monk not only that Malicoat never thought anyone would ask him such a question, but that he had indeed been talking to his dead little girl. "What do you say?" the monk asked him.

"Tessa, do you forgive me?"

An Opening for God's Grace

While Brother Vianney-Marie looked for windows through which to reach Malicoat, the prisoner warned him not to push religion too hard.

Between his visits, the monk wrote faithfully, urging Malicoat to pray for the right disposition and teaching him how to pray a perfect act of contrition. It was a painstaking three years of building confidence. "You're not there every day so you have to really pray," Brother Vianney-Marie said.

In a letter dated June 26, 2006, Malicoat informed Brother Vianney-Marie that his execution had been set for August 22 at 6 p.m. The monk's last full-length visit with him occurred on July 5. Brother Vianney-Marie referred to him, as he had often done before, as "my little Pranzini."

"Being a non-Catholic, he tried to understand. There was a nun who was praying for Pranzini. He understood the correlation there." At this point, Malicoat told Brother Vianney-Marie that he didn't mind being put to death. "He said, 'I've done things I'm not proud of. I'll have to present that to God.'"

That was just the kind of window the monk had been waiting for. "It opened it up to God's mercy." He told Malicoat that he was confiding him to the intercession of Mary and the saints, especially St. Thérèse and St. Maria Goretti, who had been murdered as a child and had forgiven her killer, who later repented.

On July 20, Malicoat's lawyers informed Brother Vianney-Marie that the inmate's family minister would not be able to attend the execution. Malicoat had agreed to have a priest and Brother Vianney-Marie assist him instead.

The monk realized that "everything is going to be possible now." He wrote Malicoat a long letter about Catholicism, "explaining the faith in a gentle way and telling him how to pray and ask for divine mercy and the forgiveness of the others he has offended."

"I told him a little bit about confession: that the priest has the faculties to absolve. It would be possible to make an act of faith in the Church. Then confess. The minimum for a Catholic that enables this vital sacrament to go ahead," he said.

Malicoat did not write back this time. It's Brother Vianney-Marie's experience that prisoners that close to death quit writing.

Enter the Confessor

Father Kirk Larkin, assistant pastor of a parish in Ponca City, Oklahoma, had done prison ministry before his ordination. That had been a while. Out of the blue, one of Malicoat's lawyers contacted him about assisting at the execution. It caught the priest off-guard.

"At first I said no," Father Larkin said. His previous work had not prepared him for anything like this. "Then I thought, 'Maybe God has called me to do this.'"

He joined Brother Vianney-Marie in taking up the burden of Malicoat's soul, and several days were added to the agony. The execution was delayed to August 31.

The Final Days

As August 31 dawned, the priest and the monk drove down to the penitentiary, arriving a little after 10:00 am, and proceeded to Death Row. Malicoat's lawyers met them with the news that they weren't sure Malicoat would confess to the priest or even see the two men.

"He was so petrified," Brother Vianney-Marie recalled. "He said, 'The last time I confessed it got me Death Row.' You just don't know the tension these guys are under."

But at 10:45 a.m., the monk and the priest were ushered in to see Malicoat. Brother Vianney-Marie had never seen him look worse. Malicoat was slumped over for terror and want of sleep.

"It's inhuman," the monk said. He was given about an hour with his last visitors, and Brother Vianney-Marie wasted no time. He made quick inquiries about Malicoat and his family and then introduced him to Father Larkin, telling Malicoat that he could make an act of faith and confess to him. He gave Father Larkin the telephone.

Malicoat told the priest he didn't want to confess.

"James was truly concerned about other people more than himself at this point," Father Larkin recalled. "He told me, 'Father, I don't want to burden you with the horrible things that I've done and that have been done to me over the course of my life.'"

The priest, with nothing rehearsed, trying to pry open the window that Brother Vianney-Marie had cracked, turned to the Profession of Faith. He went through the Creed point by point, asking Malicoat whether he agreed with each article.

Breakthrough

Brother Vianney-Marie could hear only the priest's side of the conversation. He was in agony. He got up and went to the back of the room, where he paced and prayed the rosary out of earshot.

"It was a terrible weight," Brother Vianney-Marie said. But at the same time, "I never felt so much support of prayer of others as on that day. It wasn't just me who was there. It was everyone from the monastery and many from the surrounding community who were spiritually present in prayer."

Brother Vianney-Marie looked up from his prayers to see Father Larkin raising his hand in blessing over James Malicoat. The monk had no way of knowing whether this was absolution. But he could be pretty sure.

"I just knew it was his confession," Brother Vianney-Marie said. "I was ready to jump through the ceiling."

A few minutes later and Father Larkin was beckoning Brother Vianney-Marie back to Malicoat.

"All of a sudden, he had this weight off his conscience," Brother Vianney-Marie said. "I told him, 'I don't think you're my friend, you're my brother.' He has all the same graces. I said, 'Are you ready to go?' and he said, 'Yeah.' There was a peaceful tranquility."

Brother Vianney-Marie at that point became the last friend in the world who would speak to Malicoat.

"I wanted to make sure that the last contact from the outside, which I also meant for his mother, was 'I love you.'"

The priest and the monk went on to witness the execution that evening. None of Malicoat's family was there.

"It was vulgar," Brother Vianney-Marie said. "He was pretty brave." Malicoat's last words were to ask forgiveness.

"When I was watching it I was saying, 'Jesus, Mary, Joseph save him. Take him to heaven.'"

Brother Vianney-Marie found out only later that Malicoat's death had occurred on the same date, August 31, that St. Thérèse's Pranzini had been put to death.

A few days after the execution, Brother Vianney-Marie received a letter from Malicoat dated August 29, two days before his execution. In it the doomed man had written: "You will see, prayer is never in vain."

Questions for Discussion

1. The theme of mercy has been especially prominent in the Church in recent decades, dating at least from Pope St. John Paul II's 1980 encyclical *Dives in Misericordia.* The focus has been first of all on God's mercy toward us, but then also on our duty to be "Be merciful, even as your Father is merciful."[iii] What is it about the times in which we live that makes mercy so urgent?

2. In speaking about human mercy, Pope St. John Paul II wrote in *Dives in Misericordia,* "An act of merciful love is only really such when we are deeply convinced at the moment that we perform it that we are at the same time receiving mercy from the people who are accepting it from us."[iv] What do you think he meant by this, and why is it important for the service component of this Discipleship Series?

_____

_____

_____

_____

_____

_____

_____

3. What are some of the most beautiful examples of mercy you have either personally witnessed or read or heard about? What touched you about them?

_____

_____

_____

_____

_____

_____

_____

_____

4. In calling us to forgive "seventy times seven," Jesus is
    not making forgiveness "cheap." The person who has
    clearly sinned must accept some responsibility and be
    open to receiving forgiveness, as we see over and over
    in the Gospels (Zaccheus the tax collector, the woman
    caught in adultery, the prodigal son). Pope St. John
    Paul II wrote: "In no passage of the Gospel message
    does forgiveness, or mercy as its source, mean indul-
    gence towards evil, towards scandals, towards injury
    or insult. In any case, reparation for evil and scandal,
    compensation for injury, and satisfaction for insult are
    conditions for forgiveness."[v]

But he also writes that mercy by definition goes beyond strict justice, beyond "an eye for an eye." So even
a modest opening to being sorry and receiving forgiveness can be enough. In addition, it is often hard to
assign clear blame because hurts are usually a two-
way street and merciful forgiveness is needed on both
sides.

Discuss what can be helpful in navigating this delicate
path to forgiveness. If using examples from your own
life, be discreet and careful not to betray confidences.

_____

_____

_____

_____

_____

_____

_____

_____

5. What struck you in particular from the profile of mercy, "The Monk and the Murderer"? Are you or anyone you know involved in jail or prison ministry, and if so, what insights emerge from it?

   • NOTE: It must be said that it was wrong for the state to execute Malicoat. The Church teaches that capital punishment must not be practiced where governments have other means to protect the community, such as life in prison.

_____

_____

_____

_____

_____

_____

_____

_____

Group Prayers of Intercession
8 to 10 minutes

Closing Prayer

Prayer of St. Faustina asking to be made a Channel of Mercy

O Lord, I want to be completely transformed into your mercy and to be your living reflection.

May the greatest of all divine attributes, that of your unfathomable mercy, pass through my heart and soul to my neighbor.

Help me, O Lord, that my eyes may be merciful, so that I may never suspect or judge from appearances, but look for what is beautiful in my neighbors' souls and come to their rescue.

Help me, O Lord, that my ears may be merciful, so that I may give heed to my neighbors' needs and not be indifferent to their pains and moanings.

Help me, O Lord, that my tongue may be merciful, so that I should never speak negatively of my neighbor, but have a word of comfort and forgiveness for all.

Help me, O Lord, that my hands may be merciful and filled with good deeds, so that I may do only good to my neighbors and take upon myself the more difficult and toilsome tasks.

Help me, O Lord, that my feet may be merciful, so that I may hurry to assist my neighbor, overcoming my own fatigue and weariness.

Help me, O Lord, that my heart may be merciful so that I myself may feel all the sufferings of my neighbor.

May your mercy, O Lord, rest upon me. Amen.

---

i   *Dives in Misericordia*, 13.

ii   Mt 18:21-35.

iii Lk 6:36.

iv *Dives in Misericordia*, 14.

v   Ibid.

Session 5

A Heart Set on God

> Blessed are the pure in heart, for they shall see God.
>
> **Matthew 5:8**

The Lord in His Scriptures

Approach the Lord in Purity

Who shall ascend the hill of the LORD? And who shall stand in his holy place? He who has clean hands and a pure heart, who does not lift up his soul to what is false, and does not swear deceitfully. He will receive blessing from the LORD, and vindication from the God of his salvation. Such is the generation of those who seek him, who seek the face of the God of Jacob. **Psalm 24:3-6**

The Root of Sin is in the Heart

"You have heard that it was said, 'You shall not commit adultery.' But I say to you that every one who looks at a woman lustfully has already committed adultery with her in his heart." **Matthew 5:27-28**

116

Then Pharisees and scribes came to Jesus from Jerusalem and said, "Why do your disciples transgress the tradition of the elders? For they do not wash their hands when they eat."

He answered them, "And why do you transgress the commandment of God for the sake of your tradition? For God commanded, 'Honor your father and your mother,' and, 'He who speaks evil of father or mother, let him surely die.' But you say, 'If any one tells his father or his mother, What you would have gained from me is given to God, he need not honor his father.' So, for the sake of your tradition, you have made void the word of God. You hypocrites! Well did Isaiah prophesy of you, when he said: 'This people honors me with their lips, but their heart is far from me; in vain do they worship me, teaching as doctrines the precepts of men.'"

And he called the people to him and said to them, "Hear and understand: Do you not see that whatever goes into the mouth passes into the stomach, and so passes on? But what comes out of the mouth proceeds from the heart, and this defiles a man. For out of the heart come evil thoughts, murder, adultery, fornication, theft, false witness, slander. These are what defile a man; but to eat with unwashed hands does not defile a man."
Matthew 15:1-20

Where your Treasure is, there will your Heart be

"Do not lay up for yourselves treasures on earth, where moth and rust consume and where thieves break in and steal, but lay up for yourselves treasures in heaven, where neither moth nor rust consumes and where thieves do not break in and steal. For where your treasure is, there will your heart be also."
Matthew 6:19-21

The Path to Purity of Heart

[I]n everything by prayer and supplication with thanksgiving let your requests be made known to God. And the peace of God, which passes all understanding, will keep your hearts and your minds in Christ Jesus. Finally, brethren, whatever is true, whatever is honorable, whatever is just, whatever is pure, whatever is lovely, whatever is gracious, if there is any excellence, if there is anything worthy of praise, think about these things.
Philippians 4:6-8

The Pure and Innocent See the Things of God

[Jesus] rejoiced in the Holy Spirit and said, "I thank thee, Father, Lord of heaven and earth, that thou hast hidden these things from the wise and understanding and revealed them to babes; yea, Father, for such was thy gracious will."
Luke 10:21

Soak in the Word

Two Minutes of Silence

Reflect...

This session features many short Scripture passages for reflection, but there is something obvious that joins them all – the heart. The first thing we need to understand, then, is the meaning of the word "heart" for the writers of Sacred Scripture.

For the Jewish people of both Old and New Testament times, the heart is the vital center, the core, of the human person. It is the center of desiring, choosing and willing, as well as of emotion.

In our culture we often reduce the heart to our feelings, and that is a far more superficial, sentimental, "Valentine's Day" conception. But when we say things like, "she put her whole heart into it," or "this is something really close to his heart," we are nearer to the Jewish understanding.

Brief as the Scripture passages are for this session, taken together they give us a very good picture of what God is telling us in this Beatitude. He wants us to understand that our deeds flow from the inside out. Whatever we choose to "treasure," whatever ambitions and desires we nourish by our thoughts and imagination, will shape and possess our heart, and our way of being and acting will flow from that. The outcome may be beautiful and holy, or it may be ugly and sinful. For most of us, it may be something of a mixture, requiring a lifetime of vigilance and purification.

When we read in this Beatitude that the pure of heart "shall see God," we might conclude that it simply means the pure of heart will get to heaven and see God there. Certainly it includes that, but the "seeing" begins already in this life.

By analogy, consider the observable fact that your ability to see and feel what other people are going through – your ability to empathize – depends on your willingness to go outside yourself and open your heart. A certain generosity of spirit is required. The person who is utterly self-absorbed will size up other people as objects to be used or discarded depending on their usefulness to him. He won't "see" the hopes, dreams, joys and sorrows of others, because he is too focused on himself.

We are talking, then, about a heart that is hardened and blind, rather than tender and perceptive. It is an "impure" heart, in the sense of being contaminated by selfishness. If such impurity of heart blinds one even to the things of man, imagine what it does to the things of God. If we wish to "empathize" with God, to be of one heart and mind with him, to "see" him – and to see all else through his eyes – we need a deep interior attunement and generosity of spirit. This can only come through prayer, the sacraments and a life of virtue.

When we speak of impurity, we often have sexual impurity in mind, and certainly that is one of the greatest "blinders" of the eyes of the soul. The pornography epidemic has polluted many hearts in our day, trapping people in a web of self-absorbed addiction and serious sin from which it is difficult to emerge.

But other cravings, other attachments, can blind our hearts as well — to power, to money, to fame, to comfort, etc. Unfortunately, the range of things to which we can become attached seems almost limitless. Again, as Jesus has told us, "where your treasure is, there will your heart be as well."[i]

The passage from St. Paul lays out beautifully the path to purity of heart. We must be people of prayer and supplication, and give thanks to God always. And we must focus our thoughts and desires on "whatever is true, whatever is honorable, whatever is just, whatever is pure, whatever is lovely, whatever is gracious, if there is any excellence, if there is anything worthy of praise."[ii] If we prayerfully and consciously dwell on these things, making them our "treasures," then we know that is where our hearts will be. Thus purified, we can be confident that we will experience Christ's peace and not only see God, but see the world through his eyes.

Catechism of the Catholic Church

2518 – The sixth beatitude proclaims, "Blessed are the pure in heart, for they shall see God."[iii] "Pure in heart" refers to those who have attuned their intellects and wills to the demands of God's holiness, chiefly in three areas: charity;[iv] chastity or sexual rectitude;[v] love of truth and orthodoxy of faith.[vi] There is a connection between purity of heart, of body, and of faith....

2519 – The "pure in heart" are promised that they will see God face to face and be like him.[vii] Purity of heart is the precondition of the vision of God. Even now it enables us to see *according* to God, to accept others as "neighbors."

Pope John Paul II

"[W]e find in the words of the Sermon on the Mount the reference to the heart, that is, to the interior man. The interior man must open himself to life according to the Spirit, in order to participate in evangelical purity of heart" *(General Audience, April 1, 1981).*

Pope Benedict XVI

In Jesus of Nazareth, *Pope Benedict XVI distilled the essence of that purity of heart which allows us to see God:*

"We will see God when we enter into the 'mind of Christ' (Phil 2:5). Purification of heart occurs as a consequence of following Christ, of becoming one with him. 'It is no longer I who live, but Christ who lives in me' (Gal 2:20)."[viii]

Pope Benedict goes on to write that this becoming-one-with-Christ must involve following Christ's path, which was not one of self-exaltation but rather of self-emptying, obedience, humility, sacrifice and the service of others.

The Lord in the Life of His People

The Mystical Heart of Brendan Kelly

The following article, written by Austin Ruse, tells the story of Brendan Kelly, a remarkable boy born with Down syndrome who died of leukemia at the age of 16. His short life was characterized not only by a pure heart, but also by the holy "littleness" of the poor in spirit and the meek, and the compassion of the merciful, reminding us how connected the Beatitudes are to one another. This article was posted on "The Catholic Thing" website (www.thecatholicthing. org) on June 14, 2013. It is reprinted with permission.

Two weeks before his death at sixteen, Brendan Kelly's aunt helped him into bed one night. Owing to massive steroid treatments to fight the ravages of chemo, and being a big boy anyway, he weighed more than 200 pounds. So it was difficult getting him to bed, made more difficult because large sores covered his whole body.

There was no place you could touch him that did not hurt. Except his head. She patted him there and Brendan said, "Aunt Kelly, I am so happy. All you need to be happy is to open your heart to Jesus."

A psychiatrist, who was supposed to help him through the rough patches of a lifetime of leukemia, asked him what it was like to have cancer. Brendan said, "It is like driving a car with Karen in the back seat." Karen was a panther that Ricky Bobby's father put in Ricky's back seat so he could overcome his fear of driving. Don't know the movie Talledega Nights? Brendan knew every line.

The psychiatrist ended up not charging for many of Brendan's visits. She said, after he died, that talking to Brendan was like talking to God. And how could she charge for something like that? She also said his death was the hardest event of her life.

A Compassionate Heart

Brendan possessed a supernatural ability to spot pain in others and to move in like a surgeon to fix it. Brendan's mother coached girls' baseball. One girl on the team came from an abusive home. She was mean, uncommunicative. Brendan laid siege, sitting with her, putting his head on her shoulder, talking to her, trying to make her laugh, talking about Jesus.

This went on for weeks. At first she hated it. Eventually, she smiled, then laughed, then utterly transformed into a new person, which she remains today. Such things happened all his life.

Brendan was born with Down syndrome. At four, doctors diagnosed him with leukemia, a cancer with a high rate of remission – but the treatment is devastating. They turn a fire hose of chemo into your body and then pump you up with massive doses of steroids. This can go on and off for months and with terrible effects.

A Wish Comes True: Meeting St. John Paul II

After his diagnosis, his family applied to the Make-a-Wish Foundation: he wanted to meet the pope. Make-a-Wish didn't quite believe him since only one other child had ever asked for that. So they met with him privately, tempted him with Disney World, a submarine ride, baseball stars. They wanted to make sure meeting the pope was his wish and not his parents'. Brendan insisted.

In September 2001, the family gathered with others at Castel Gandolfo waiting to meet John Paul II. When the pope entered, rather than wait his turn, Brendan broke and ran to the pope and stood holding his arm as he greeted all the other pilgrims. Brendan would not move and the pope loved it. He kept glancing at Brendan and smiling.

As the pope began to leave, indeed when he was out the door and around the corner, Brendan shouted out, "Good-bye Pope." John Paul the Great returned and the family snapped a picture of the smiling Pope reaching down to take Brendan's hand.

Talking to Jesus

Brendan was a mystic. He carried on a continuous conversation with Jesus and his Guardian Angel. After confession one evening, he made an extended penance. Outside, his father asked what took him so long, and Brendan said he was talking to Jesus. "In the tabernacle?" his father asked. "No, in the light above the tabernacle." Except, according to Father Alexander Drummond, the Church was utterly dark.

Brendan would not pass a church without blowing a kiss and shouting, "Hi, Jesus." So normal and natural was this that a priest of Opus Dei still sermonizes about this as an advanced state of the interior life.

So in love was he with the Eucharist that after chemo, when he had to be isolated because his immune system was ravaged, the family would sit outside the church in their massive black Suburban. At Communion, Father Drummond would walk down the aisle, leave the church, and go outside. Brendan's window went down and the priest would give him the Blessed Sacrament.

"I Love You, Bella"

Brendan suffered with leukemia nearly his entire life. He got it at 4 and underwent two-and-a-half years of treatment. It returned at age 10 with another two years of treatment. At 14, it came again and he underwent a bone marrow transplant.

He offered all his pain for others. Among his special intentions was Bella Santorum [daughter of Rick Santorum, the former Senator from Pennsylvania]. Because of her own devastating disability, she should have died within hours of birth. In intense pain Brendan would shout, "I love you, Bella." Bella still lives.

There are many remarkable stories about Brendan Kelly. One day his father received an urgent email from a colleague who had been taken hostage by terrorists in Mumbai. He asked for Brendan's prayers. Brendan prayed and said the man would be rescued. That he was rescued that very night is less interesting than, at a moment of abject terror, he asked for the intercession of the boy with Down syndrome and leukemia.

Brendan was a normal boy. He loved sports and movies, and sometimes showed a scatological sense of humor. He did not want to be sick – or die – and wondered why God answered all his prayers except those for himself. He sometimes suffered anxiety and even depression. Father Drummond says Brendan was willing to carry even these as the Cross.

When Father Drummond asked if he wanted to be an altar boy, Brendan immediately said yes. Told he would have to wear a cassock and surplice, he got a faraway look in his eyes and whispered, "I love those."

Young Brendan departed this world for the next on April 27, 2013. He was buried in his cassock and surplice. Brendan Kelly, pray for us.

Questions for Discussion

1. This session includes quite a few Scripture passages
   that relate to our theme of purity of heart. Point to a
   couple of them that especially strike you and discuss
   why.

_____

_____

_____

_____

_____

_____

_____

_____

2. What do you think are the greatest obstacles in to-
    day's world to having a pure heart? What are the keys
    to acquiring and maintaining a pure heart?

_____

_____

_____

_____

_____

_____

_____

3. In a world in which unborn children with a Down syndrome diagnosis are aborted at a horrific rate (nearly 100% in Iceland, 98% in Denmark, at least 67% in the U.S.), the story of Brendan Kelly is especially compelling. What insights or lessons do you think people should draw from that story?

_____

_____

_____

_____

_____

_____

_____

_____

4. Does reaching out in charity to your neighbor in need contribute to purity of heart? Or does purity of heart contribute to reaching out in charity to your neighbor in need? Or is it both? What is the connection? Discuss the reason for your answer.

_____

_____

_____

_____

_____

_____

_____

_____

5. When people decide they want to grow in purity of heart, do you suspect they mostly think of attitudes and habits they need to *eliminate,* or attitudes and habits they need to *build?* Certainly an honest appraisal will reveal that both are necessary, and one person's situation is often quite different from another's. But in general, do you have a sense of which should be prioritized? If so, why?

_____

_____

_____

_____

_____

_____

_____

Group Prayers of Intercession

8 to 10 minutes

Closing Prayer

Psalm 51:3-10

Have mercy on me, God, in accord with your merciful love;

In your abundant compassion blot out my transgressions.

Thoroughly wash away my guilt;

And from my sin cleanse me.

For I know my transgressions;

My sin is always before me.

Against you, you alone have I sinned;

I have done what is evil in your eyes

So that you are just in your word,

And without reproach in your judgment.

Behold, I was born in guilt,

In sin my mother conceived me.

Behold, you desire true sincerity;

And secretly you teach me wisdom.

Cleanse me with hyssop, that I may be pure;

Wash me, and I will be whiter than snow.

You will let me hear gladness and joy;

The bones you have crushed will rejoice.

Turn away your face from my sins;

Blot out all my iniquities.

A clean heart create for me, God;

Renew within me a steadfast spirit.[ix]

Session 5 - *A Heart Set on God*

i   Mt 6:21.

ii   Phil 4:8.

iii Mt 5:8.

iv Cf. 1 Tim 4:3-9; 2 Tim 2:22.

v   Cf. 1 Thess 4:7; Col 3:5; Eph 4:19.

vi Cf. Titus 1:15; 1 Tim 1:3-4; 2 Tim 2:23-26.

vii Cf. 1 Cor 13:12; 1 Jn 3:2.

viii Joseph Ratzinger. *Jesus of Nazareth*. (NY: Doubleday, 2007) 95.

ix New American Bible, copyright 1991, 1986, 1970, Confraternity of Christian Doctrine, Inc., Washington, D.C., and used by permission of the copyright owner. All Rights Reserved. No part of the New American Bible may be reproduced in any form without permission in writing from the copyright owner.

Session 6

"Peace I Leave with You; My Peace I Give to You"

> Blessed are the peacemakers, for they shall be called sons of God.
>
> **Matthew 5:8**

The Lord in His Scriptures

Peace Comes from on High

How beautiful upon the mountains are the feet of the one bringing good news, announcing peace, bearing good news, announcing salvation, saying to Zion, "Your God is King!"

Listen! Your sentinels raise a cry, together they shout for joy, for they see directly, before their eyes, the LORD's return to Zion. Break out together in song, O ruins of Jerusalem! For the LORD has comforted his people....[i]
Isaiah 52:7-9

Live in Harmony

[L]ove one another with brotherly affection; outdo one another in showing honor. Never flag in zeal, be aglow with the Spirit, serve the Lord. Rejoice in your hope, be patient in tribulation, be constant in prayer. Contribute to the needs of the saints, practice hospitality.

Bless those who persecute you; bless and do not curse them. Rejoice with those who rejoice, weep with those who weep. Live in harmony with one another; do not be haughty, but associate with the lowly; never be conceited. Repay no one evil for evil, but take thought for what is noble in the sight of all. If possible, so far as it depends upon you, live peaceably with all.

Romans 12:10-18

Indwelling Spirit

"...I will pray the Father, and he will give you another Counselor, to be with you forever, even the Spirit of truth, whom the world cannot receive, because it neither sees him nor knows him; you know him, for he dwells with you, and will be in you....

...Peace I leave with you; my peace I give to you; not as the world gives do I give to you. Let not your hearts be troubled, neither let them be afraid."

John 14:16-17, 27

[T]he fruit of the Spirit is love, joy, peace, patience, kindness, goodness, faithfulness, gentleness, self-control.... If we live by the Spirit, let us also walk by the Spirit.
Galatians 5:22-23, 25

God's Children

Beloved, we are God's children now; it does not yet appear what we shall be, but we know that when he appears we shall be like him, for we shall see him as he is.

We know that we have passed out of death into life, because we love the brethren. He who does not love abides in death. Anyone who hates his brother is a murderer, and you know that no murderer has eternal life abiding in him.

By this we know love, that he laid down his life for us; and we ought to lay down our lives for the brethren.

But if anyone has the world's goods and sees his brother in need, yet closes his heart against him, how does God's love abide in him? Little children, let us not love in word or speech but in deed and in truth.
1 John 3:2, 14-18

Soak in the Word

Two Minutes of Silence

Reflect...

How elusive is peace! Not only is it hard to achieve, it is difficult to define. Often we tend to think of it simply in terms of the absence of conflict and noise. What mother of small children does not long for "a moment's peace" in the middle of her hectic day!? And then there is the soldier in battle who yearns for the end of the war, or at least a cease-fire.

But peace is much more than that. In Hebrew the word is *Shalom,* while in the Aramaic spoken by Jesus it would have been *Shlama.* Both include not only our typical sense of peace as tranquility, but a state of wholeness, perfection, complete wellbeing – having all that is good.

A "peacemaker," then, is someone who helps foster this fullness of harmony and wellbeing in those around them.

But we must remember who is using the word here, in this Beatitude. It is Jesus, the one who said, "Peace I leave with you; my peace I give to you; *not as the world gives do I give to you."* [ii]

The second part of that sentence matters. Jesus is telling us that we need to recalibrate our sense of peace, so that the fullness of tranquility and wellbeing are not measured according to the world's terms. He tells us he will give us *his* peace, the peace of the God-man who was persecuted, mocked and hung on a cross.

This doesn't mean that Jesus' peace is really anguish. No, it is the deepest, most powerful sense of tranquility and wellbeing imaginable. But it must necessarily be able to coexist with the suffering of the cross. And at its heart it must be born of complete self-giving *love*.

How can this be possible for mere mortals like us? There is only one way, and that is by God's grace, by the indwelling of his Holy Spirit, which makes us truly his children.

Read the Scripture passages again. It's all there. Yes, the peace of Christ *does* include getting along harmoniously with other people, being kind and patient, showing mutual respect. But it goes so much deeper than that, calling for a level of grace-filled, loving self-sacrifice that is willing to suffer, even unjustly, laying down one's life for one's brethren.

Recall the second part of this Beatitude. The peacemakers are blessed – why? Because "they shall be called sons of God" (alternatively translated "children of God").

There you have it. The blessing comes in being joined to God, sharing his lifeblood – sharing both cross and Resurrection out of *love* – to the point where we will be able to say with St. Paul, "[I]t is no longer I who live, but Christ who lives in me; and the life I now live in the flesh I live by faith in the Son of God, who loved me and gave himself for me."[iii]

Session 6 - "Peace I Leave with You"

The peace of the children of God is, in the end, the only peace worth having. It is not just tranquility. It is fullness of life in every respect, contagious in its joy. If we have that peace, joined to Christ, indwelt by the Holy Spirit, miracles of peace will happen around us, just as they did in the life of St. Teresa of Calcutta, exemplified in the story below.

Then we will be blessed peacemakers, indeed.

Catechism of the Catholic Church

2305 – Earthly peace is the image and fruit of the peace of Christ, the messianic "Prince of Peace."[iv] By the blood of his Cross, "in his own person he killed the hostility,"[v] he reconciled men with God and made his Church the sacrament of the unity of the human race and of its union with God. "He is our peace."[vi] He has declared: "Blessed are the peacemakers."[vii]

Pope John Paul II

Through Christ's great peacemaking act—his Sacrifice on the Cross—we have become his brothers and sisters, and, with him, heirs of eternal life. Because of this new relationship of ours with God in Christ, *peace is now possible:* peace in our hearts and in our homes, peace in our communities and in our nations, peace throughout the world. Yes, Jesus Christ is the supreme Peacemaker of human history, the Reconciler of human hearts, the Liberator of humanity, the Redeemer of man. He is our peace[viii] *(Mass for Peace, Manila, Philippines, February 19, 1981).*

Pope Benedict XVI

Peace is a gift of God and at the same time a task which is never fully completed.... I invite all those who wish to be peacemakers, especially the young, to heed the voice speaking within their hearts and thus to find in God the stable point of reference for attaining authentic freedom, the inexhaustible force which can give the world a new direction and spirit, and overcome the mistakes of the past *(Message for the World Day of Peace, January 1, 2011).*

Pope Francis

While weapons traffickers do their work, there are poor peacemakers who give their lives to help one person, then another and another and another; for such peacemakers, Mother Teresa is a symbol, an icon of our times.[ix] Last September, I had the great joy of proclaiming her a Saint *(Message for the World Day of Peace, Jan. 1, 2017).*

The Lord in the Life of His People

An Impossible Peace

Being a peacemaker may be blessed, but it is not for the faint of heart. That is what we learn from the following story from the life of St. Teresa of Calcutta. We also learn of God's provident care for those who place their trust entirely in him as they seek to do his will.

It is August 1982. In Lebanon, West Beirut is being decimated by the Israeli-Palestinian conflict, with air and ground bombardments being carried out by the Israeli military.

Hidden in the thick of the violence, a poignant human drama is unfolding. Thirty-seven Muslim children with disabilities lie abandoned in an orphanage. They are trapped, helpless and running out of food, and the orphanage may be obliterated at any moment.

The Missionaries of Charity, with two houses in northern Lebanon, learn of this desperate situation, and word reaches Mother Teresa. She does not hesitate; the children must be rescued, and she will come to Beirut to lead the effort.

Mother Teresa takes a ferry from Cyprus to the coastal city of Jounieh, Lebanon, because the Beirut airport has been bombed. She boards the ferry carrying a candle, explaining, "This is a candle to Our Lady of Peace. When we get to Beirut we are going to light this candle, and we will have peace."[x]

All for Jesus

Before continuing from Jounieh south to Beirut, Mother Teresa speaks with a priest and an officer, telling them of her intention to enter the war zone in order to bring the abandoned children to safety. Her conversation is filmed by a woman who has been traveling with Mother Teresa to produce a documentary. The dialogue goes like this:

Mother Teresa: "I feel the Church must be present at this time, because we are not into politics. This is why we need to be present."

Priest: "That's a good idea, but you must understand the circumstances, Mother.... Two weeks ago a priest was killed. It's chaos out there. The risk is too great."

Mother Teresa: "But Father, it is not an idea. I believe it is our duty. We must go and take the children one by one. Risking our lives is in the order of things. All for Jesus. All for Jesus. You see, I've always seen things in this light."

Into the War Zone with Our Lady of Peace

Having now arrived in East Beirut, Mother Teresa stands before President Ronald Reagan's special envoy to the Middle East, Philip Habib. It is August 13. She tells him they must go tomorrow to rescue the trapped children, assuring him that she has prayed to Our Lady. "I asked for a cease-fire for tomorrow, the eve of her feast day" [the eve of the feast of the Assumption].

Habib — a veteran diplomat renowned for his work in Vietnam — listens respectfully but then replies, "Mother, I am more than happy to have a woman of prayer at my side. I believe in the power of prayer; I believe that prayer is answered. I am a man of faith. But, you see, you're asking Our Lady to deal with Prime Minister Begin, and do you not think that the time limit you gave him is a little short? You should extend it a little?"

"Ah, not at all, Mr. Habib! I'm sure we'll have a cease-fire tomorrow."

To which Habib replies, "If we get a cease-fire, I personally will ensure that arrangements are made for you to go to West Beirut tomorrow."

Rescue in the Quiet Dawn

To the surprise of everyone but Mother Teresa, a cease-fire agreement is suddenly reached and the morning of August 14 dawns quietly. A convoy of ambulances, vehicles of the International Red Cross, passes into West Beirut, carrying Mother Teresa, Red Cross and hospital workers, and a group of sisters. Mother has even persuaded Israeli medical personnel to contribute supplies to the effort.

As she enters the orphanage, Mother Teresa's wrinkled face beams with a smile. One by one, she begins to embrace the children, who are huddled in a group on the floor. They range in age from 7 to 21, and many are deformed or mentally retarded. Some begin to cry, and she comforts them. They are put into four Red Cross vehicles and taken to a convent run by the Missionaries of Charity in Mar Takla in East Beirut. There they are lovingly washed, clothed and fed.

At a news conference later that day, Mother Teresa refuses to discuss the politics of the Lebanese crisis and simply says, "The children are with us. They are being treated."

A relief worker present at the orphanage at the moment of the rescue would later be more effusive in her description of the scene, recalling that while some of the children were profoundly disabled, both physically and mentally, others were simply passive and stunted from neglect: "Mother Teresa took [them] in her arms, and suddenly, they flourished, becoming somebody else, like when one gives a little water to a wilted flower. She held them in her arms and the children bloomed in a split second." [xi]

Questions for Discussion

1. What is peace? Is it a feeling? A set of circumstances socially or politically? A spiritual state? Is it a symptom or fruit of something deeper? Is it a combination of some or all of these? Discuss, bearing in mind the points of reference in this session.

_____

_____

_____

_____

_____

_____

_____

_____

2. A cynic reading the story of St. Teresa of Calcutta's rescue of 37 children during a brief cease-fire in Beirut might argue that this was a mere drop of peace in an ocean of violence that has plagued the Middle East since long before 1982, violence that continues in our own day and that shows no sign of ending anytime soon. So what significance does that have, really, in the scheme of things, other than making us feel good for a moment? How would you respond?

_____

_____

_____

_____

_____

_____

_____

3. St. Teresa of Calcutta once wrote: "Keep the joy of loving the poor and share this joy with all you meet. Remember, works of love are works of peace." How does your love and service toward your neighbor in need bear the fruit of peace?

_____

_____

_____

_____

_____

_____

_____

_____

4. "Jesus Christ is the supreme Peacemaker of human history." This is part of the quote from Pope St. John Paul II in this session. But what about the fact that Jesus overturned the tables of the moneychangers in the Temple and had harsh words for many of the Scribes and the Pharisees? How do these things fit together?

_____

_____

_____

_____

_____

_____

_____

_____

5. When you think of "peacemakers," who comes to mind and why? You may think of people who are or have been well known, but also people in your own family or community.

_____

_____

_____

_____

_____

_____

_____

_____

6. What are one or two things you could do to be a maker of peace in yourself and for others?

_____

_____

_____

_____

_____

_____

_____

_____

Group Prayers of Intercession

8 to 10 minutes

Closing Prayer:

Make Me a Channel of Your Peace

Lord, make me a channel of your peace, that
  Where there is hatred, I may bring love;
  Where there is wrong, I may bring the spirit of forgiveness;
  Where there is discord, I may bring harmony;
  Where there is error, I may bring truth;
  Where there is doubt, I may bring faith;
  Where there is despair, I may bring hope;
  Where there are shadows, I may bring light;
  Where there is sadness, I may bring joy.
Lord, grant that I may seek rather
  To comfort than to be comforted;
  To understand than to be understood;
  To love than to be loved;
  For it is by forgetting self that one finds;
  It is by forgiving that one is forgiven;
  It is by dying that one awakens to eternal life. Amen.

Note: This beloved prayer, popularly but incorrectly attributed to St. Francis of Assisi, first appeared in a little French magazine in 1912. Its author is unknown. It is prayed daily by St. Teresa of Calcutta's Missionaries of Charity.

Session 6 - "Peace I Leave with You"

i   New American Bible, copyright 1991, 1986, 1970, Confraternity of Christian Doctrine, Inc., Washington, D.C., and used by permission of the copyright owner. All Rights Reserved. No part of the New American Bible may be reproduced in any form without permission in writing from the copyright owner.

ii   Jn 14:27.

iii   Gal 2:20.

iv   Isa 9:5.

v   Eph 2:16 J.B.; cf. Col 1:20-22.

vi   Eph 2:14.

vii   Mt 5:9.

viii   Eph 2:14.

ix   Meditation, "The Road of Peace", Chapel of the Domus Sanctae Marthae, 19 November 2015.

x   Ann Rodgers, "Mother Teresa revered for putting others first." *Pittsburgh Post-Gazette.* Oct. 7, 2007.

xi   Fady Noun, "Mother Teresa, the war in Lebanon and the rescue of 100 orphans and children with disabilities," Sept. 2, 2016. http://www.asianews.it/news-en/Mother-Teresa,-the-war-in-Lebanon-and-the-rescue-of-100-orphans-and-children-with-disabilities-38470.html.

Appendix

Suggestions for Service

As stated in the Introduction, we are not truly disciples of Christ until we take seriously his words: "Truly, I say to you, as you did it to one of the least of these my brethren, you did it to me" (Matthew 25:40).

With a smile and an open heart, we are called to be the hands and feet of Christ in the world, especially to those in need. But sometimes we need a little help getting started. Here are a few suggestions:

Ask your pastor about needs in the parish community—

"Charity begins at home," and in the life of the Church that's your parish. Your pastor can help you learn who are the lonely, the elderly, the sick or homebound in your community. He can tell you who needs Holy Communion, the human kindness of a visit, and who has material needs. You might also ask if there are parishioners who need a ride to Mass because of age, health, or special needs.

Contact Catholic Charities—

Consider offering some volunteer time

to Catholic Charities, which has agencies throughout the country. To find one near you, visit ***www.catholiccharitiesusa.org.***

Check your Yellow Pages listings under "Social Service Organizations" or "Volunteer Services"—

You may be surprised to learn how many opportunities for service exist in your community: Meals on Wheels, Habitat for Humanity, Birthright or other crisis pregnancy centers, food pantries, homeless shelters, Catholic Worker houses, and more.

Pay attention to what is "right under your nose"—

Sometimes we can get tied up in a knot trying to decide where to go and what to do, when there's an elderly neighbor next door or a nursing home a few blocks away. No doubt, there are people close by that are lonely and would love a visit.

May the ancient witness be renewed: "See how they love one another!"

Photo Credits

Session 1, page 30

Blessed Solanus Casey © Mahatma Gandhi (Own work) [CC BY-SA 3.0 (https://creativecommons.org/licenses/by-sa/3.0)], via Wikimedia Commons
https://commons.wikimedia.org/wiki/File%3ASolanuscasey.jpg

Session 5, page 125

Brendan Kelly with Pope St. John Paul II © Maura Kelly. Used with permission.

Session 6, page 146

St. Teresa of Calcutta © 1986 Túrelio (via Wikimedia-Commons), 1986 /, via Wikimedia Commons
https://commons.wikimedia.org/wiki/File%3AMotherTeresa_090.jpg

The Discipleship Series

Novo Millennio Press